GUERRILLA HUNTERS
IN
CIVIL WAR
MISSOURI

JAMES W. ERWIN

Charleston London

THE
History
PRESS

Published by The History Press
Charleston, SC 29403
www.historypress.net

Copyright © 2013 by James W. Erwin
All rights reserved

Cover image: painting by Don Troiani, www.historicalimagebank.com.

First published 2013

Manufactured in the United States

ISBN 978.1.60949.745.3

Library of Congress CIP data applied for.

Contents

Acknowledgements

I wish to thank Ben Gibson and everyone at The History Press for the opportunity to realize a dream I have had since I was eight years old: to write about the Civil War. In the preparation of this book, I have received valuable assistance from, in no particular order: Dorris Keeven-Franke at the St. Charles County Historical Society; Sean Visintainer, curator, Herman T. Pott National Inland Waterways Library at the St. Louis Mercantile Library at the University of Missouri–St. Louis; and Deborah Wood, museum curator, Wilson's Creek National Battlefield. I owe a debt to Verona—sorry I did not get your last name—who told me of a story that, serendipitously, was confirmed by documents from Margie Heppermann Summers. Peter Cauchon provided valuable books and encouragement. And I cannot thank my mapmaker, Colter Sikura, enough for producing maps on a short deadline.

I also wish to acknowledge my parents, Juanita and Charles Erwin. My profound regret is that they did not live to see the book published. Mom instilled a love of reading and research. Dad patiently drove a kid all over southwest Missouri and northwest Arkansas looking for battlefields years before they were marked, armed only with a musty history book and a state highway map.

Finally, my wife, Vicki—by the example of writing her own books—showed me the dedication and hard work necessary to bring this work to fruition. I owe her so much more than I can put into words.

Prologue

Amanda Sawyer was almost home. She boarded the Hannibal & St. Joseph train early that morning in Palmyra, Missouri, on the other side of the state. It was now almost 11:00 p.m., and the train had left Easton, just a few miles from St. Joseph. She would be home in Kansas tomorrow. It would be good to be home, as well as to get back to teaching.

Also on the train were Barclay Coppoc and Sidney Clarke. Coppoc, a lieutenant in the Kansas infantry, had been a member of John Brown's band that attacked Harper's Ferry in 1859. He had been left at the base to guard the group's supplies and escaped the post-attack pursuit. Clarke was a personal secretary to Kansas senator (now General) James H. Lane, a prominent antislavery politician and a leader of the Jayhawkers in prewar Kansas.

The Hannibal & St. Joseph's service had been intermittent at best over the last few months. Armed men had taken shots at passing trains, and service to St. Joseph was suspended altogether the weekend before this trip because it was unclear who exactly, Unionists or Secessionists, controlled the city. But federal troops there had been ordered to Lexington to oppose General Sterling Price, and on August 30, Secessionists rushed in to occupy St. Joseph. That very evening, their commanders were being fêted at the Patee Hotel.

What Sawyer, Coppoc, Clarke and the others on the train did not know was that a group of a dozen armed men had been scouting the railroad for days, and on this day, September 3, 1861, the men decided to strike.

First, the guerrillas chased away the railroad's section hands, who were supposed to keep watch over the bridge and track to make sure that it was in good repair. They also threatened the local residents, who might have given the alarm that something was afoot. Then the guerrillas set fire to the supports of the bridge. It weakened them to the point that the bridge would collapse, but the engineer could not see that—especially at night—until it was too late.

The locomotive got about halfway across the 160-foot bridge before the supports gave way, and it crashed into the Platte River thirty-five feet below. The freight, mail and baggage cars plunged down, and the two passenger cars followed, piling one on top of the other. "Quicker than I thought," Clarke recalled, "I found myself buried beneath a mass of ruins." The passengers were thrown into a heap at the front of the cars, some crushed by the bridge's timbers, others cut by jagged glass and others still trapped in the debris. Amid the shrieks of pain and screams of terror, Abe Hager, a baggage man, one of the few uninjured, tried to pull those who were still alive onto the banks of the river. After rescuing as many as he could from the bloody scene, Hager made his way to St. Joseph to summon assistance. According to witnesses, three or four armed men watched silently from above on the western abutment but offered no help.

Fifteen passengers, including Coppoc, and five trainmen were killed. Sawyer and Clarke survived, among the dozens who were injured.

Up to this point, the bridge burning and a few shots fired into trains constituted a relatively low level of violence. The attacks could be justified as being against military targets. The Union commanders were concerned with them, but the public was more focused on the activities of the conventional armies at Wilson's Creek (and at Bull Run in the East). But this tragedy on the Platte River was the first to involve a large loss of civilian lives. It dispelled any notion that civilians could remain neutral in the war or that guerrillas could be defeated by moral suasion or threats to confiscate noncombatants' property.

To combat this threat, Governor Hamilton Gamble needed reliable troops who were capable of hunting down the guerrillas. He found them in men like George Wolz, Aaron Caton, John Durnell, Thomas Holston and Ludwick St. John. You have likely never heard of them. They are not listed among the heroes of the Civil War. They did not lead any famous charges or win any medals. They did not get to march in the Grand Army of the Republic parade in Washington, D.C., after the defeat of the Confederacy.

These men served as privates in a cavalry regiment. They spent most of their time in camp and on scouts looking for guerrillas. It was a hard life, and over three years of the war, these boys (for most were in their teens and early twenties) became hard men. Combat, when it came, was often short, sharp, brutal and unforgiving. In Missouri, neither side showed much mercy for defeated foes.

The guerrillas who terrorized Missouri during the Civil War were colorful men dressed in gaudy "guerrilla shirts" and plumed hats. Their daring and vicious deeds brought them a celebrity never enjoyed by the Federal soldiers who hunted them. Many books have been written about the exploits of William Quantrill, "Bloody Bill" Anderson, George Todd, Tom Livingston and other "noted guerrillas." But in the end, men like Wolz, Caton, Durnell, Holston and St. John killed Anderson, Todd and Livingston and defeated the rest. They were just five of the anonymous thousands of Union soldiers who fought in the guerrilla war, whose participation has largely been forgotten with the passage of time. This is their story.

Chapter 1

"The Wolf by the Ears"

"A Reprieve Only"

Missouri had been a literal and figurative battleground since its birth. It was admitted to the Union as a state in 1821, but only after a bruising two-year controversy over slavery that was settled by the admission of a free state, Maine, thus preserving a precarious racial balance between North and South. The Missouri Compromise provided that subsequent states created from the Louisiana Purchase above the southern boundary of Missouri—the 36° 30' north parallel—would be free states, and those south of the line would be slave states. Thomas Jefferson feared that "this is a reprieve only, not a final sentence." He regretted the existence of slavery, "but as it is, we have the wolf by the ears, and we can neither hold him, nor safely let him go. Justice is in one scale, and self-preservation in the other."

The Missouri Compromise postponed for three decades the thorny legal and political issue: could the federal government condition the admission of a state based on whether it allowed or prohibited slavery? And so, slave and free states were admitted in pairs until the next great accession of territory after the Mexican-American War. In one fell swoop, the United States acquired not only Texas but also land that stretched all the way to the Pacific Coast that would eventually become the states of New Mexico, Arizona, Utah, Nevada and California. But this new bounty resurrected an old problem: what would be the status of slavery in these newly acquired territories when they became states?

After a four-year struggle, Congress hammered out a deal that—again temporarily—preserved the Union. Texas was admitted as a slave state, California was admitted as a free state (even though it was largely south of the 36° 30' parallel) and slavery was kept in the District of Columbia but the slave trade was barred there. A strengthened Fugitive Slave Law was also enacted.

"BLEEDING KANSAS": PRECURSOR TO WAR

The Compromise of 1850 had a short life. Senator Stephen Douglas (among many others) was anxious to prepare the way for a transcontinental railroad. His preferred route was from Chicago through the Nebraska Territory, a vast region that included what is now Kansas, Nebraska and parts of Colorado, Montana and the Dakotas, much of which had been set aside for Native Americans who were displaced from their homes in the East. All of it lay north of the Missouri Compromise line, and so before any part could be admitted as a state, there had to be an accommodation with the Southern slavery interests.

Douglas's solution was popular sovereignty. "[A]ll questions pertaining to slavery in Territories, and in the new States to be formed therefrom, are to be left to the people residing therein," thereby effectively repealing the Missouri Compromise. Northern antislavery activists vowed to "engage in competition for the virgin soil of Kansas" and quickly organized settlers to claim Kansas as a free state. Proslavery partisans met the challenge. South of Kansas City, the border was an imaginary line on the prairie. All Missourians had to do was to cross it and stake their claims. Hundreds poured into Kansas to do just that.

There was a cultural as well as a political divide between the eager settlers. New Englanders regarded their western neighbors crude and uncouth "pukes." They mocked westerners' dialect: "I had to learn...that a pail was bucket, afternoon was evening, sunrise was sunup, bread was light bread, hot biscuits was bread, [and] Johnny cake was cornbread." They were derided in antislavery newspapers as "Border Ruffians," a "lawless mob...drunken, bellowing, bloodthirsty demons...wearing the most savage looks and giving utterance to the most horrible imprecations and blasphemies; armed, moreover, to the teeth with rifles, revolvers, cutlasses, and bowie-knives." Proslavery men, though, embraced the name of Border Ruffians. Missouri senator David Atchison declared them to be "men of property, of education—the best kind of men. We are the men who will submit to no wrong."

Missourians considered the eastern migrants as effete, "mostly ignorant of agriculture, picked up in cities and villages, they of course have no experience as farmers, and if left to their unaided resources—if not clothed and fed by the same power which has effected their transportation—they would starve." They came to know Kansans by a name, "Jayhawkers," that later would evoke fear and hate for their fierce attacks on persons and property.

The early elections in Kansas were plagued by fraud, with most of the votes coming from Missourians—some in armed bands—who took up "residence" the night before. In 1855, electoral tensions boiled over into outright violence. Proslavery man Franklin Coleman killed his neighbor, Charles Dow, over a property line dispute. One of Dow's antislavery friends threatened Franklin and was arrested by the proslavery sheriff, Samuel Jones. Antislavery partisans broke him out of jail, and the two sides, including Border Ruffians led by Senator Atchison, squared off against each other for two weeks before dispersing without further violence.

But the following year, provocation followed provocation to inflame the debate over slavery. On May 21, United States Marshal Israel Donalson, backed by eight hundred Missourians led by the ubiquitous Atchison, stormed Lawrence to arrest antislavery activists accused of ambushing Sheriff Jones. The Border Ruffians burned the Free State Hotel, destroyed two abolitionist newspapers and threw their type into the river. On May 22, Senator Preston Brooks of South Carolina attacked and severely injured Senator Charles Sumner of Massachusetts on the floor of Congress by beating him with a cane in retaliation for his delivery of a fiery address, titled "The Crime Against Kansas," in which he had vilified Brooks's relative, Senator Andrew P. Butler of South Carolina. The country was in an uproar.

On May 24, John Brown hacked five proslavery men to death on Pottawatomie Creek. The massacre set off a summer of retaliatory violence. Atchison led about 1,500 Missourians into Kansas to "clean out" the area south of Lawrence. One of his columns split off to attack Osawatomie, the home of John Brown and his family. In the ensuing battle, one of Brown's sons was killed. Four other antislavery residents of the town also died. The Missourians lost two killed, but they leveled Osawatomie.

The new territorial governor, John W. Geary, finally managed to curtail the fighting with the help of the United States Army. There were still sporadic bursts of violence as jayhawkers raided into Missouri and Missourians retaliated, but the border settled into relative peace.

Dred Scott, Harper's Ferry and the Southwest Expedition

All Dred Scott wanted was his freedom. He had been taken from Missouri by his owner to live in Illinois and the Minnesota Territory, both free. And so Scott filed suit in 1846 in Missouri state court upon his return to St. Louis. The petition alleged that he had been assaulted and falsely imprisoned. These were the customary allegations because there was no direct cause of action to gain a declaration that one was free. If the jury found the plaintiff to be free, then he had been assaulted and falsely imprisoned; if found to be a slave, then it was merely chastisement of the owner's "property." The matter languished in the state courts for years. Finally, a jury found Scott to be a free man. His owner appealed to the Missouri Supreme Court. Had the case been tried twenty years earlier, Scott would clearly have won because under Missouri law (and the law generally in slave states), a slave taken to live in a free state or territory became emancipated as a matter of law. But Scott was swept up in the increasingly divisive issues of the day. In a split and frankly political opinion, the court held that Scott's status reverted to that of a slave upon his return to Missouri.

Scott took his claim to federal court. He lost again and appealed to the United States Supreme Court. Once again, there was a long delay, and once again his lawsuit became entangled in the national controversy over slavery. Finally, the court issued its decision in 1857. Chief Justice Roger B. Taney wrote that Scott could not bring a lawsuit in federal court because no Negroes, slave or free, were considered citizens of the United States. Moreover, Scott's residence in Minnesota did not make him a free man because Congress lacked the power to prohibit slavery in the territories, and therefore the Missouri Compromise was unconstitutional. The decision outraged Republicans and antislavery forces. The *Dred Scott* case, in historian Don E. Fehrenbacher's words, provided "a new stimulus for political rhetoric at a time when Kansas seemed to have run out of 'outrages.'"

Dred Scott. Scott was a Missouri slave who was taken by his master to free states and territories. His lawsuits filed in Missouri courts seeking freedom were caught up in the sectional crisis. Ultimately, the Supreme Court declared that slaves were not citizens and that the Federal government lacked the power to prohibit slavery in territories. The decision reignited the political firestorm over slavery after the violence in Kansas had abated. *Library of Congress.*

Within two years, though, the slavery debate was further exacerbated when, in the early morning of October 17, 1859, John Brown and a party of black and white raiders struck at the armory in Harper's Ferry, Virginia. Brown held out in the firehouse for thirty-six hours until his men were killed or captured by United States marines under the command of Colonel Robert E. Lee. Brown was swiftly tried and hanged. In his death, he became a martyr to the abolitionist cause and a symbol of fear to slaveholders.

The presidential election of 1860 saw the country split along sectional lines. Abraham Lincoln carried only states north of the Ohio River, as well as California and Oregon. John Breckinridge, the proslavery Democratic candidate, carried eleven of the fifteen slave states. John Bell, the Constitutional Union candidate, carried three border states. Stephen Douglas, the Northern Democratic candidate, barely carried Missouri with 35.5 percent of the vote and split New Jersey with Lincoln.

Lincoln received only 10 percent of the Missouri vote, mostly from a strongly antislavery German immigrant population in St. Louis. In the Missouri River counties where most of Missouri's slaves lived, Lincoln's

The firehouse at Harper's Ferry, Virginia. John Brown led a group of black and white raiders against the armory at Harper's Ferry on October 17, 1859. They barricaded themselves in this firehouse for thirty-six hours, until they were captured or killed by United States marines led by Colonel Robert E. Lee. Brown was tried and hanged. He became a martyr to the antislavery cause. *Library of Congress.*

support was negligible. There was no secret ballot in Missouri. Voters announced their choice orally in front of anyone who cared to attend the polling place. As a result, those who dared to vote for Lincoln were known to everyone. In Lexington, the local newspaper published the names of Lincoln voters and suggested that they find residence elsewhere. Several did.

The secession crisis was coming to a head, with states of the Deep South preparing to hold conventions to vote on whether to leave or remain in the Union. Meanwhile, in response to residents' "urgent appeals" from southwest Missouri for protection from antislavery raiders led by James Montgomery, Governor Robert Stewart called out the militia to patrol the border with Kansas. General Daniel Frost led the Southwest Expedition, six hundred men from St. Louis and Jefferson City, to northwestern Bates County to "defend the western border."

In the meantime, General William S. Harney, the commander of the Department of the West, sent Captain Nathaniel Lyon to Fort Scott with orders to arrest Montgomery and other free state "outlaws." Lyon was an abolitionist himself known for his antislavery essays and a secret member of the Wide Awakes, a loosely organized paramilitary group that acted as "political police" in support of the Republican Party.

On December 6, Lyon met Montgomery in secret. Lyon found him to be "a man of great earnestness of purpose." They concocted a scheme by which Lyon could avoid court-martial: Montgomery would leave to visit a friend before the soldiers arrived to arrest him. As Lyon's biographer noted, it "worked to perfection." Montgomery was gone long before the soldiers reached his place.

After two weeks, Frost decided that the militia was not needed. One of his lieutenants, John S. Bowen, proposed that he stay on the border that winter with three companies of infantry and an artillery battery. Frost agreed. Bowen's men, styled the Southwest Battalion, built a blockhouse near Balltown, drilled every day and patrolled throughout the brutally cold winter. In January 1861, Bowen had a pleasant meeting with Lyon at Fort Scott, completely unaware that peace had been restored through Lyon's scheme with his quarry. In the same month, the men of the Southwest Battalion returned home.

Chapter 2

"Lucifer...Moved Hell Itself" to Missouri

"This Means War!"

Missouri's new governor, Claiborne Fox Jackson, a former Border Ruffian, favored secession. In January 1860, he sent an emissary to the commander of the St. Louis Arsenal to confirm that the muskets, cannons and ammunition stored there would be available to the state in the case of an invasion. Jackson's lieutenant governor, Thomas C. Reynolds, organized Minutemen, paramilitary troops pledged to take measures "as shall be deemed necessary for our mutual protection against the encroachment of Northern fanaticism and the coercion of the Federal Government."

Unionists were also concerned about the safety and availability of the stores at the arsenal in the event of war. Frank Blair Jr., a U.S. Congressman and brother of Lincoln's postmaster general, raised his own paramilitary group, the "Home Guards," mostly German American immigrants in St. Louis, to counter Secessionist Minutemen. He also successfully sought to have Nathaniel Lyon transferred to St. Louis, along with a company of regulars, to take command of the arsenal.

Jackson convinced the proslavery legislature to call for election of delegates to a convention to consider secession. At a meeting in the Mercantile Library in St. Louis on March 4 (the day Lincoln was inaugurated), the convention voted ninety-eight to one to remain in the Union. But war could not be avoided. On April 12, 1861, Confederate forces bombarded Fort

Captain (later General) Nathaniel Lyon. Lyon, an avowed abolitionist, was assigned to St. Louis at the request of Frank Blair, the leading Missouri Unionist politician. Lyon's aggressive actions confirmed the secessionists' worse fears about a Federal "invasion" of the state. On August 10, 1861, Lyon was killed at the Battle of Wilson's Creek. *Library of Congress.*

Sumter. The country's—and Missouri's—four-year nightmare began.

On April 15, President Lincoln called on the states for 75,000 volunteers, including 3,123 from Missouri. On April 17, Jackson fired back his response: Missouri would not furnish one man for this "illegal, unconstitutional and revolutionary…inhuman and diabolical" requisition. Secessionists seized the arsenal at Liberty, Missouri, on April 20. On April 21, the Federal government directed Lyon to muster into service four regiments of Blair's Home Guards.

Matters became even tenser when Governor Jackson ordered the militia under General Daniel Frost to Camp Jackson to undergo "training" near St. Louis. Lyon suspected that they had designs on the arsenal. On May 10, Lyon surrounded the camp with the German Home Guards and captured the Missouri militiamen. That was provocative enough, but while Lyon's troops were marching the prisoners to town, someone in the crowd of civilians watching the procession fired at his troops. The Federals returned the fire. Before the mêlée was over, twenty-eight had been killed. When news of the "Camp Jackson Affair" reached Jefferson City, the legislature acted immediately to authorize the creation of the Missouri State Guard, with Sterling Price, a Mexican-American War veteran, as its commander.

On June 11, Jackson and Price met Lyon and Blair in St. Louis to try to come to an accommodation. Lyon refused any deal that would restrict

John C. Frémont. Frémont was known as the "Pathfinder" for his exploration of the West and was the first Republican presidential candidate. As commander of the Department of Missouri, he declared the state subject to martial law. Although severely criticized and investigated for corruption, he managed to arm Missouri state troops, albeit with obsolete or obsolescent weapons. *Library of Congress.*

Federal troop movements with the state. "[R]ather than concede to the State of Missouri the right to dictate to my government in any matter, however unimportant," Lyon declared, "I would rather see you…and every man, woman, and child in the state, dead and buried. This means war!"

Lyon swiftly forced the Missouri State Guard to withdraw to southwest Missouri. It camped at Wilson's Creek about ten miles southwest of Springfield, where it was joined by Confederate troops under Ben McCulloch. Although outnumbered, Lyon was nothing if not bold. On the night of August 9, Lyon led one column to Wilson's Creek, and Franz Sigel led another to take the Confederates from the rear. The plan nearly succeeded the next morning. But Sigel's men were routed, and when the Confederates turned their entire force against Lyon, he was killed leading a counterattack. The surviving Union officers realized that retreat was their only option. And retreat they did, eventually all the way to Rolla, the railhead of the Southwest Branch of the Pacific Railroad and Union supply base.

The triumphant Price marched north to the Secessionist stronghold of Lexington, where, after a three-day siege, he captured a large Union force. Price's success was short-lived, however, as the new Union commander in Missouri, John C. Frémont, the former Republican presidential candidate, ponderously and belatedly began to move against him. Price withdrew once again to southwest Missouri. Although he tried to get McCulloch and other Confederate commanders to join in attacks against the Federals, they all refused. Formal military operations stalled.

In November, the Secessionist remnants of the Missouri legislature met at Neosho and passed an ordinance of secession. But Missouri's functioning civil government was firmly in the hands of the Union. In July, the convention that met to consider secession approved a provisional government and vacated the state offices held by Claiborne Jackson and others elected in 1860. They chose Hamilton Gamble, a St. Louis lawyer—former member of the Missouri Supreme Court and leader of the anti-secession forces in the March convention—as the provisional governor. The members of the convention acted as a legislature until the 1864 election.

"I NEVER IMAGINED I WOULD BE AN OFFICEHOLDER UNDER ABE LINCOLN"

While the actions of conventional forces settled the question of whether Missouri would effectively be able to secede from the Union, the first stirrings of a guerrilla war started at the same time. The presence of a large Confederate army in the state initially contributed to keeping guerrilla activity to a minimum, especially compared to the levels reached later. There were no large guerrilla bands that roamed the countryside and hid out in the brush. Union commanders were nevertheless concerned with sporadic actions in which men would appear to burn railroad bridges, tear

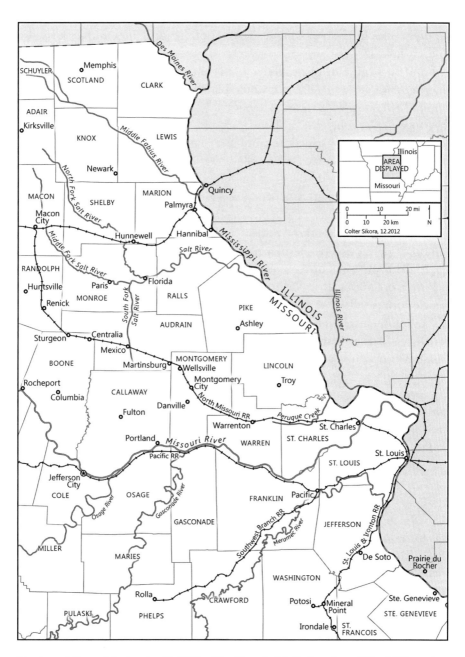

Northeast Missouri during the Civil War. The Hannibal & St. Joseph and North Missouri Railroads were important transportation links threatened by guerrillas throughout the war. Joseph Porter crisscrossed this region to recruit Confederate soldiers until he was defeated at Kirksville in 1862. *Map by Colter Sikora.*

up the tracks, fire into passing trains or cut telegraph lines and then return to their farms.

From the beginning of hostilities, both sides recognized the significant role that railroads and the telegraph would play in the war. Armies could use the railroad to transport men and supplies across great distances at a relatively fast speed. Certainly the railroads, despite their frequent derailing and sometimes flimsy construction, were a far better method of transportation than using hundreds of wagons pulled by horses or oxen over the unpaved, often rutted and muddy roads of the time. The telegraph made it possible for commanders to send orders and receive reports almost instantaneously. The distinct advantages of the new technologies of war made them prime targets for roaming bands of raiders and a drain on Union resources when hundreds or thousands of men had to be diverted from the battlefield to guard the army's line of communications from guerrillas.

The most important rail link was the Hannibal & St. Joseph Railroad, which connected those two towns in north Missouri. It was a major line of communication between the eastern United States and the states and territories of the West. Early in the war, a short line between West Quincy, Missouri (opposite Quincy, Illinois), was extended to connect to the Hannibal & St. Joseph at Palmyra, Missouri. This shortened communications with the East even further because Quincy had a direct connection to Chicago. (No bridge spanned the Mississippi between Missouri and Illinois until after the war.)

The North Missouri Railroad ran from St. Louis to the Missouri River opposite St. Charles. Passengers and freight were transported across the river by ferry, and the rails continued from St. Charles to a connection with the Hannibal & St. Joseph at Hudson (also known as Macon City, or Macon). The North Missouri passed through parts of Little Dixie, a stronghold of slavery and Secessionist sentiment. It was the subject of frequent attacks during the war.

The Pacific Railroad ran south of the Missouri River from St. Louis through Jefferson City. At the beginning of the war, the Pacific Railroad was extended to Warrensburg. It would not be completed to Kansas City until late 1865. The Southwest Branch of the Pacific Railroad diverged at Franklin (now Pacific) and ran through the hills of central Missouri to Rolla. Although some grading for new tracks was completed for a few miles west of Rolla, and though more than one Union commander urged the extension of the Southwest Branch, its railhead remained at Rolla throughout the war. The final line was the St. Louis and Iron Mountain, running into southeast

John Pope. Pope tried to combat attacks on railroads in north Missouri during 1861 with threatened assessments against committees of known secessionists that were supposed to control the guerrillas. The scheme failed. Pope accurately predicted that the guerrilla war would require that small detachments of Union troops be scattered throughout the state, where without proper discipline by their officers, matters would become inflamed by "political feelings and personal hostility." *Library of Congress*.

Missouri between those two towns. It was not extended into Arkansas until after the war.

Union commanders began to complain of attacks on trains and bridges north of the Missouri River in July and August 1861. The new commander in north Missouri, General John Pope, condemned the "wanton destruction" of bridges and culverts that threatened to shut down the railroads. The attackers were freelance bands of men that would strike and then melt back into the population. When the Union soldiers questioned the locals about who was responsible, they claimed to know nothing—whether from fear, political loyalty or just a desire to remain neutral. Pope issued a proclamation that he would hold the inhabitants of towns and villages within five miles of any destruction financially accountable unless they could provide "conclusive proof of active resistance" or "immediate information…giving names and details" to the army.

Pope's warning was followed shortly by an order directing that the civilian population in each county seat and town appoint a committee of public safety that would be responsible for maintaining order and invested with the power to call out the citizens to fight "small parties of lawless marauders." He would send troops if requested, but the commanding officer would levy assessments against the town or county requesting them sufficient to pay the soldiers' expenses.

Civilians protested bitterly against Pope's orders and did their best to avoid being named to one of the committees. One prominent citizen of Montgomery County, William "Uncle Billy" Martin, was just the sort that Pope thought had the most to lose and had the most influence over the nascent guerrilla movement. Before the war, Martin contributed a considerable amount of land to the North Missouri Railroad for a depot, which in return named the depot Martinsburg. Uncle Billy asked his old friend, the railroad's president, Isaac Sturgeon, to accompany him to an interview with Pope, during which he hoped to be removed from the list of those who would be held answerable for any bridge burning or other depredations.

They met Pope at his quarters in Mexico, Missouri. Uncle Billy made his plea, protesting ill health among other reasons. Uncle Billy pointed to his companion. "There is my friend Mr. Sturgeon," he said. "He can tell you." Pope turned to Sturgeon, who paused and said, "If I had a matter I wanted well attended to, Uncle Billy would be *the* man I would select." Pope laughed, but Uncle Billy was dumbfounded, saying, "Is this the way you are going to help me?" The general told him that the position was one that should not be sought, but it could not be declined. Defeated, Uncle

Billy shook his head and said, "I never imagined I would be an officeholder under Abe Lincoln."

Pope told them to see Colonel Ulysses S. Grant, the local commander, and that he would approve any action Grant wanted to take. Uncle Billy told Grant that if he gave Uncle Billy the power to name three persons in his place to keep the peace, he would make sure that the fellows committing the attacks would "stand around now." Grant agreed, and they went to see Pope with the solution. Pope offered each man a "very fine" cigar worth twenty-five cents. When Grant remarked that a general could afford better cigars than a colonel, Pope told him to take a handful, and he did.

Pope's committees did little to stop the attacks on trains. In the first week of August, guerrillas fired into Hannibal & St. Joseph trains several times near Palmyra and briefly raided the town. Pope responded by sending six hundred men, who took what they needed for rations from the stores and told the owners to bill the county. They seized John McAfee, the Speaker of the House of Representatives from the prior legislature, and set him to work digging trenches and rifle pits in one-hundred-degree weather. As a final indignity, the Union commander ordered McAfee tied to the top of a locomotive. The engineer refused. Nonetheless, these Union activities, as much as the attacks by guerrillas, kept northeast Missouri in turmoil. J.T.K. Hayward, the president of the Hannibal & St. Joseph, warned, "If we cannot have a change in the administration of military affairs here in North Missouri our cause will be ruined."

On the evening of August 16, guerrillas fired on a Hannibal & St. Joseph train carrying soldiers of the Sixteenth Illinois Infantry as it left Palmyra and again at Hunnewell. One man was killed and another wounded. Confederate guerrillas fired into a train again on August 18, but no one was hurt in this attack. Pope viewed the attacks as a test of his resolve to carry out the assessments threatened in his proclamation. He directed that the local commander give the citizens of Palmyra and Marion County six days in which to turn over the guilty persons or have $10,000 in money or property confiscated from the county and $5,000 from the town.

Although Pope claimed that he did not have "the slightest disposition to play the tyrant to any man on earth," leading citizens saw it differently, one protesting that Pope's policies "might do in a foreign country, but I do not think it can be done here, without alienating friends and making the feeling more bitter on the part of enemies." Twelve prominent men from the area asked General Frémont to intervene and prohibit enforcement of the assessment in Marion County and Palmyra because Pope's order "proposes to impose penalties prescribed by no law, civil, criminal, or military" and punishes "the innocent with the guilty—Union men with disunionists." After a meeting with Frémont and bending to political pressure from Governor Gamble, Congressman Blair and others, Pope grudgingly rescinded his order authorizing assessments against civilians who failed to prevent attacks by guerrillas.

At the end of August, the guerrilla war turmoil continued in the northeast quarter of Missouri, Confederate troops were about to occupy St. Joseph in the northwest, Confederate armies threatened the southeast corner of the state and General Price had driven Federal troops out of southwest Missouri and was advancing on the Union garrison at Lexington. General Frémont proclaimed martial law throughout the state. He threatened to shoot anyone caught under arms against the Union, including those "who shall be proven to have destroyed...railroad tracks, bridges, or telegraphs." The proclamation also provided that the slaves of all persons who took up arms against the United Sates "are hereby declared freemen."

Frémont did not consult either President Lincoln or Governor Gamble before taking this action. Indeed, both learned of it from newspaper accounts. Lincoln responded immediately, directing Frémont not to allow anyone to be shot for Rebel activities without his express approval. Lincoln also asked the general to delete the paragraph about confiscating property and freeing slaves out of concern that it would turn "our Southern Union friends" and the state of Kentucky, then wavering between the Union and the South, "against us." Frémont refused to modify the proclamation without a direct public order to do so, which the president was forced to give.

On September 3, guerrillas wrecked the Hannibal & St. Joseph train as it crossed the Platte River west of Easton, killing twenty and injuring more than one hundred, almost all of them civilians. Cutting the railroad was an obvious military benefit to Confederate arms because it severed an important transportation link that would not be fully restored for weeks. At the time, General Price was approaching the federal post at Lexington. But neither General Price nor anyone else among Secessionist officers admitted ordering its destruction. It was the work of irregular forces—guerrillas operating without supervision or orders from regular Southern authorities.

The tragedy on the Platte River was the first to involve a large loss of civilian lives. It crystallized an attitude among Northerners toward irregular warfare that Kansans had held for years. The *New York Times* called for "summary vengeance [to] be speedily visited upon the assassins." Secessionists were not just Rebels fighting for a cause, however misguided, another Northern

This North Missouri Railroad locomotive, the I.N. Sturgeon, named for the president of the line, is shown at St. Charles waiting for cars to be ferried across the Missouri River. The North Missouri was a key transportation link connecting St. Louis to the Hannibal & St. Joseph Railroad and to western Missouri. It was also a frequent target of guerrillas, including Bill Anderson's attack on Centralia in 1864. *St. Charles County Historical Society.*

paper raged, but the agents of "Lucifer [who], to get a more congenial and sympathetic clime, has moved hell itself to that portion of the State where they undermine railroad bridges…all from pure love of murder."

Union commanders stationed troops at key points along the railroads to protect them from further attack. Many of the Home Guard companies that were raised in various towns were assigned to guard bridges. They had even less training and poorer equipment than the volunteer regiments in Federal service.

The guerrillas made one last push in December to disrupt railroad communications. Under orders from General Price (or so they later claimed), more than five hundred men led by a former University of Missouri professor, James Searcy, gathered in groups of forty or fifty for a Christmas attack on the North Missouri Railroad. Spies told Union commanders of the planned attack. General Henry Halleck, the new commander in Missouri, fired off a series of telegrams ordering troops from Hermann, Jefferson City and St. Charles County to converge on the railroad between Hudson and Warrenton with directions to kill or capture the bridge burners. The troops trying to cross the Missouri River were hampered by ice and a lack of ferryboats. The units north of the river had to contend with snow six inches deep. They found the bridges at Warrenton, the Cuivre River, Salt River and Davis Fork (near Mexico) damaged. The Confederates also burned the bridges at Sturgeon and Centralia and tore up the track at Renick. Union troops stationed along the Hannibal & St. Joseph farther west reported that guerrillas had burned the railroad's spans across the Chariton River (both 150 feet long) and at Bucklin and Callao.

Union soldiers captured a number of the bridge burners, but the damage was extensive. The North Missouri Railroad later reported that its losses included not only the bridges but also the loss of eight thousand railroad ties, more than thirty railroad cars damaged or destroyed and a depot and a water tank burned to the ground. Service was not restored to Hudson until January 13.

Halleck issued an order that accused anyone who destroyed railroads or telegraph lines of being "guilty of the highest crime known to the code of war." He directed that those caught in the act be shot immediately and those accused of such crimes (but not caught in the act) be tried by a military commission and, if found guilty, to be executed. Halleck further directed that the slaves of all Secessionists in the vicinity of the damage—and the Secessionists themselves and their property, if necessary—be pressed into service to make repairs. He also reinstituted the practice of levying assessments against neighboring towns and counties to pay the cost of the repairs. In a letter to Senator Thomas Ewing Sr., Halleck wrote that he would likely be cast as a blood-thirsty monster in the press for these measures, but he said with evident frustration, "Our army here is almost as much in a hostile country as it was when in Mexico…It must be done; there is no other remedy. If I am sustained by the Government, well and good; if not, I will take the consequences."

Chapter 3

"A Military Force for Suppressing the Rebellion"

AN ALTERNATIVE TO "WORSE THAN USELESS" TROOPS

The Union forces raised in Missouri were a hodgepodge of Home Guards, battalions, companies and other units that seemed to spring up spontaneously, eventually totaling 241 companies and 22 independent battalions.

While at Jefferson City, then colonel Ulysses Grant found that

> *volunteers had obtained permission from the department commander, or claimed they had, to raise, some of them, regiments; some battalions; some companies—the officer to be commissioned according to the number of men they brought into service. There were recruiting stations all over town, with notices, rudely lettered on boards above the doors, announcing the arm of service and length of time for which recruits at that station would be received.*

Some units served unpaid. Few received any training, and their weapons and equipment (to the extent they had any at all) generally consisted of whatever they brought with them from home.

This system could not endure. To replace these troops, Governor Hamilton Gamble called for forty-two thousand volunteers to serve as the Six Month Militia. Only about six thousand men enlisted, and even these men were poorly armed, poorly trained and notoriously undisciplined.

Hamilton Gamble. As a member of the Missouri Supreme Court, Gamble cast the lone dissenting vote in favor of Dred Scott's freedom. He was selected as the provisional governor in 1861 and served until his death in 1864. Gamble negotiated an agreement with President Lincoln for the creation of the Missouri State Militia to be armed, fed and paid by the Federal government but to be employed only in Missouri. *Wilson's Creek National Battlefield.*

The commander at Pacific, Missouri, for example, wrote that the Six Month Militia regiment stationed there was "worse than useless" and not worth the cost of rations to feed them. He could not even use them to guard the railroad or bridges, let alone chase the enemy.

Even as he called for the Six Month Militia, Gamble was looking to President Lincoln for a better solution. He wrote to Lincoln on August 26, 1861, and personally visited him a few days later to make his case. Gamble pointed out that the state lacked the money to properly raise and equip a militia force. (It had $21,000 in the treasury.) Nearly one-third of the state was under Confederate control, and the local civil authorities were either hostile to the Union or nearly helpless to carry on basic, ordinary governmental activities such as collecting taxes. Gamble blamed radical Home Guards raised by Lyon and Frémont for the constant friction with civilians. He also complained that out-of-state troops lacked any understanding of conditions in Missouri. For one thing, they were from free states and found the institution of slavery distasteful if not immoral. Gamble proposed enlisting a state militia that would be paid by the Federal government. These men would be charged with hunting the guerrillas, and this would release for service in the armies confronting the main

Confederate forces elsewhere the thousands of regular volunteer troops from Missouri and other states now performing that duty.

Frémont got wind of the proposal and telegraphed Lincoln requesting that Gamble not be given authority to raise regiments in Missouri. Upon his return to Missouri, Gamble met with Frémont at his sumptuous St. Louis headquarters. Gamble noted that Lincoln had directed Frémont to give all possible aid in recruiting and equipping the state militia and once again suggested that state troops would be more effective in fighting the guerrillas because of their familiarity with the area and the Rebels themselves. The meeting ended inconclusively. Gamble went back to Frémont's headquarters the next day, but the general snubbed him and Gamble left in a huff for Jefferson City.

In October 1861, the state convention met and approved the issuance of Union Defence Bonds in the amount of $1 million to pay for military expenses. It approved the organization of a Missouri state militia and, by resolution, directed Gamble to return to Washington to reiterate his proposal for the creation of a state militia paid and equipped by the Federal government. On November 4, Gamble met with the president. Lincoln asked him for more specifics. Gamble sat down that night and wrote a proposal that he gave to the president the next day. It called for a "force to serve within the State as Militia during the war." It was "not to be ordered out of the State, except for the immediate defense of the State of Missouri," and it was "to be armed, equipped, clothed, subsisted, transported and paid by the United States." Lincoln approved the plan for "a military force…for suppressing the rebellion," with the proviso that its commanding officer be the same person appointed by the Federal government to command the department in which Missouri was located. Gamble was given the power to select the field-grade officers—colonels, lieutenant colonels and majors—but the men elected the captains and lieutenants who commanded the companies. The agreement was duly embodied in General Order No. 96 issued by the War Department.

In accordance with the agreement, Gamble appointed Brigadier General John Schofield—the Union commander of the Department of Missouri—as a brigadier general and commander of the Missouri State Militia (MSM). Recruitment began in January 1862 but quickly ran into an administrative snag. The army bureaucracy in Washington decreed that the Federal government would not subsist, pay or clothe any member of the MSM until the company to which the soldier was assigned was mustered in, and that could not be done until it reached a strength of at least eighty-three men. Once again, Gamble made a trip to Washington to make a personal plea to carry out the agreement with Lincoln "in spirit." He was successful, and men were mustered in singly as they enlisted.

Recruiting for the MSM went much better than that for the Six Month Militia. Although the Union army itself discouraged the recruitment of cavalry as volunteer regiments (because they were so expensive to equip and difficult to train), the nature of the enemy and the terrain dictated that most of the MSM serve in cavalry, or at least units that were mounted (even if they generally fought dismounted). The guerrillas were highly mobile and heavily armed. Their preferred tactic was already known to be the ambush, followed by their retreat into the "brush." Infantry could never catch them and could, at best, provide only a passive defense for fixed installations such as bridges, blockhouses or towns.

And so by June 1862, the state had raised fourteen cavalry regiments, two independent cavalry battalions, one infantry regiment and two artillery batteries—about 13,500 men in all. The infantry and artillery performed garrison work throughout the war. The burden of being the guerrilla hunters in Civil War Missouri fell on the MSM cavalry.

Missouri's financial and equipment problems seemed solved by the Lincoln-Gamble agreement as embodied in General Order No. 96. But Congress stepped in and limited the number for which the Federal government would pay to ten thousand men. This necessitated a reorganization and consolidation of the existing units. And so in early 1863, the cavalry regiments were expanded from ten to twelve companies, and five cavalry regiments—the Third, Tenth, Eleventh, Twelfth and Fourteenth—were broken up, their men assigned to other units. One regiment, the Fifth Cavalry MSM, and one of the cavalry battalions were mustered out altogether. A new Third Cavalry was formed from elements of the Tenth and Twelfth Cavalry. The Thirteenth Cavalry, renumbered the Fifth Cavalry, added the remaining companies of the Twelfth.

"THIS MASS OF FURNITURE"

George Wolz was born on May 30, 1842, at his parents' farm in Grundy County, Missouri, fourteen miles northeast of Trenton. Conrad and Maria Wolz, among the first permanent white settlers in Grundy County, came from Prussia. George had an older brother, John, and three sisters, Elizabeth, Catherine and Mary.

George enlisted as a private in Company I, Third Cavalry MSM, at Chillicothe, Missouri, on March 17, 1862, a little over two months before his twentieth birthday. Company records show that he was mustered in (i.e., formally enrolled) to military service "for the war in MO."

George Wolz and the Third Cavalry MSM remained at Chillicothe until mid-May 1862. While there, they received their uniforms, weapons and other accoutrements. Available records do not specify what training the men received, but most likely it was limited to dismounted drill and perhaps some simple mounted maneuvers. During this time, it was not uncommon for officers elected to lead their fellow civilians to consult a military handbook at night and then try to implement the drill they read about the next day with the men.

Federal cavalrymen were issued a dark blue canvas-lined jacket, wool shirts, flannel long johns and trousers with the seats heavily reinforced. Initially, cavalrymen were issued Hardee or "Puritan" hats—wide-brimmed hats with tall conical crowns. They might have company or regimental badges.

The cavalrymen were supposed to turn up the brim on the left side and attach a black plume. Most cavalrymen preferred a slouch hat or the forage cap.

This unidentified sergeant is armed with a LeFaucheux revolver. The LeFaucheux was the only revolver carried by Union troops to fire a self-contained metal cartridge rather than a cap and ball. It is known to have been issued to some men in the Ninth Cavalry MSM. This soldier is wearing the Hardee or "Puritan" hat, with crossed sabers and a plume on the left side (the image is reversed), as required by regulations. *Library of Congress.*

Sergeants and corporals wore inverted "V" stripes on the sleeves of their coats, three for a sergeant and two for a corporal, to indicate their rank. Officers had shoulder straps on their coats. There was little care taken to make sure that the issued clothing fit. One recruit wrote, "Coats, trousers, and other clothes were piled up in separate heaps, and each man was just thrown the first garment on top of the heap, he took it and walked away. If it was an outrageous fit, he would swap with someone else, if possible, otherwise he got along the best he could."

Fully equipped, the cavalry trooper carried a rifle, a heavy revolver, a box of cartridges, a box of percussion caps, a canteen, perhaps a haversack for rations, a tin coffee cup and numerous personal articles that he may have purchased or been given by family, such as sewing kits, pens or pencils, paper, envelopes, pictures and the like. Stephen Starr noted that horses carrying excessive weight could create severe problems on a march. One cavalryman, with tongue in cheek but with evident concern, said, "This mass of furniture, with saddle, would weigh in most cases seventy pounds…To the uninitiated it was a mystery how the rider got onto the saddle."

But the clothing the Missouri militia wore was hardly uniform, other than the blue jacket or coat—necessary to distinguish a Union soldier from a guerrilla. Even the blue coat was commonly worn by guerrillas, who found them not only comfortable but also a useful disguise. And it is doubtful that the MSM had all of the "standard" equipment because even the regular volunteer cavalry, especially in the West, rarely received everything for which the regulations called. The soldiers adapted and frequently found better (if makeshift) solutions. For example, two gunnysacks tied together and slung over the saddle was a much better way of carrying their own food and forage for their horses than the haversack.

The MSM cavalrymen were recruited mostly from rural areas of northern and central Missouri, not just because of the Unionist sentiment there but also, likely, because soldiers from such areas could supply their own horse and "horse equipments," such as saddle, saddle blanket, bridle, currycomb and brush. The men who brought their own horse and equipment to war were paid an extra forty cents per day for the "risk" of their use. The government provided cavalrymen a nose bag, a picket pin and a lariat. By 1862, Union cavalry began to be issued a shelter half, which would be kept under the saddle and over the saddle blanket on the march. Two soldiers could button them together and prop them up with poles to provide a tent. They could also be used as a roof for winter huts or as blankets.

Stephen Starr noted that the weapons issued to cavalrymen tended to be poorer as one went farther west. The weapons issued to the Missouri State Militia were the poorest of all. They received a mishmash of obsolete, obsolescent and downright antique arms. The same regiment would have several different types of firearms, making supplying them difficult. The most extreme example was the First Cavalry MSM, which, as late as 1864, had sixteen different types of breechloaders and nine different types of muzzleloaders and shotguns. The Sixth Cavalry MSM reported that its 1,109 men had 633 Austrian Lorenz muskets, 633 revolvers, 320 sabers, 25 pistol carbines, 202 pairs of "holster" pistols (single-shot muzzleloaders) and 50 cavalry musketoons.

Most MSM regiments received the Austrian Lorenz musket, a rifle originally bored for a .54-caliber ball but rebored to a .58 caliber to accept the standard rifle ammunition of the Union army. It was a single-shot weapon that had to be loaded by tearing open a paper cartridge containing the powder and ball, pouring powder down the muzzle, then ramming home the ball and paper wad on top of it, cocking the hammer, placing a percussion cap on a nipple, aiming and firing. It was not a simple or speedy process, especially in the excitement of battle. The Lorenz had a mixed reputation. Some units thought them "rough but good and reliable," while others noted that the Austrian rifles "were still in the hands of those men who had not the hardihood or ingenuity to lose them." The Missouri inspector general criticized the Austrian rifles as "of a very inferior quality and kind for Cavalry service":

> *They are too long, unwieldy and heavy for guerrilla warfare by the mounted soldier in the rapid pursuit of the enemy, without great risk of being himself disarmed by his piece becoming entangled in the undergrowth, or wrenched from his grasp in passing at a rapid pace over the uneven surface of the ground…They cannot be loaded expeditiously or fired with any degree of accuracy by the mounted trooper.*

The Ninth Cavalry MSM had the Harper's Ferry rifled musket, a better arm than the Lorenz. Like the Lorenz, it was "ineffective for cavalry service," the regimental commander concluded, "but probably the best for the particular service for which the Missouri State Militia was intended."

A few regiments, such as the Fourth Cavalry MSM, received some Hall carbines. The Hall carbine was a breech-loading weapon that evolved from an 1811 design. It was used by the Army Dragoons in the 1830s. At the opening of the Civil War, the government had five thousand Hall carbines stored as obsolete. A few entrepreneurs bought them for $3.50 each and, while they were still in the armory, sold them to General Frémont for $22.00 each. The resulting furor contributed to the decision to relieve Frémont of his command in Missouri.

The Hall carbine had a side lever that opened the breech at the top to receive the ammunition. The soldier loaded the cartridge into the breech, closed it, put a percussion cap on the nipple and fired. It was not well liked. The inspector general's primary criticism was that the top-loading breech tended to leak gas into the face of the shooter when fired, "causing the men involuntarily to start, thus affecting the accuracy of the aim."

Some MSM regiments had the Wesson carbine, a two-triggered rifle with no stock under the barrel. It was loaded by pulling the hammer to half-cock, pulling the front trigger to break open the breech and loading a .44-caliber rimfire cartridge. The breech was closed and the rifle fired with the rear trigger.

This unidentified sergeant (the rank is shown by the three chevrons on his sleeve) is holding a Savage .36-caliber revolver. The Savage was a first crude attempt at a double-action revolver. The weapon was cocked and the cylinder turned by pulling the lower trigger with the middle finger. The soldier fired it with the upper trigger. The Savage was issued in large numbers to the men of the Missouri State Militia. *Library of Congress.*

For close-in work, the MSM relied on the revolver. But the MSM revolvers, like its rifles, were a motley collection. Many, such as the Third Cavalry MSM, were given the Savage "figure 8," a clumsy .36-caliber cap-and-ball revolver. It had two triggers, one above the other. Instead of cocking the weapon with his thumb, a soldier cocked the weapon and turned the cylinder with his middle finger using the lower trigger; the upper trigger fired it. Like the two-triggered rifle, it took some coordination to fire, and a soldier could easily forget the correct sequence in the excitement of battle. Other units received the Remington revolver or the .41-caliber LeFaucheux revolver. The LeFaucheux was the only Union revolver that fired a self-contained metal cartridge, rather than a cap and ball.

It did not take long for the MSM cavalry to learn that a single revolver was not enough. Many men bought their own handguns to supplement or replace the government-issued ones. Guerrillas carried as many as four, or even six, revolvers. The Union cavalry emulated them. A trooper might have a Savage in his holster, a Colt or Remington in his belt and one or two other revolvers strapped to his saddle. This, plus his rifle, gave him some firepower that had a chance to match the guerrillas in a close-range fight.

Whether the cavalrymen were actually proficient in the use of their firearms is open to doubt. Most soldiers in the Union army, of all branches, did not receive any particular training in firing their weapons. Few took any target practice. Cavalrymen rarely fired their weapons during training while mounted to accustom their horses to the sound of gunfire, a problem that could lead to losing control of the animal during its first combat. Revolvers, in particular, are notoriously difficult to shoot accurately from the ground, let alone from a charging horse. One Union cavalryman wrote that "with revolver in hand, the trooper was more likely to shoot off his horse's ears, or kill his next comrade, than kill an enemy, however near." Regardless of marksmanship, handguns provided the volume of fire at close range needed to fight guerrillas.

As a consequence, the MSM—and Union cavalry in general in all theaters—rarely fought while mounted. As Samuel Baird of the Second Missouri Cavalry ("Merrill's Horse") explained, "When we went into a skirmish, we dismounted and went on foot, and were counted off by fours, 1-2-3-4-1-2-3-4. Number one held the horses and the other three went to the fight." One Union veteran said that men accustomed to fight on foot could deploy in this fashion in two minutes from the moment the command "Prepare to fight on foot" was given.

The first (and deadliest) enemy Missouri troops faced was disease. After leaving Chillicothe for its first post in southwest Missouri, George Wolz's regiment was hit by an epidemic of measles at Sedalia. The sick men continued with the regiment to Springfield, where several later died.

The spread of measles among the Third Cavalry was not unusual. Newly recruited troops routinely suffered from this and other "childhood" diseases, such as mumps and scarlet fever. A life in tents and exposed to the elements made respiratory diseases run rife. Sanitation in the camps was poor. Human and animal waste was not properly disposed of. Moreover, the soldier's diet left much to be desired. The standard ration of hardtack—a nearly inedible cracker whose consistency lived up to its name—was a staple while on the march. The government also provided salt pork and beans. One surgeon said that "beans killed more than bullets." A meal of bean soup often led to an outbreak of diarrhea. The soldiers fried everything, which also led to extensive digestive ailments.

Another significant problem resulting from a poor diet was scurvy, which was the third leading cause of death among soldiers after dysentery and diarrhea. Of course, the soldiers were also subject to malaria, typhoid fever, typhus and other diseases that were common in the wet and swampy areas of the state. Many were not vaccinated against smallpox, prompting repeated calls from the regimental surgeons for vaccines. The supply of medicines was frequently uncertain, particularly for units serving at a distance from major supply bases. Where there were no railroads—and everything had to be transported by wagons over rutted and muddy roads, such as those leading from Rolla into southwest Missouri—supplies of any kind were often difficult to come by reliably.

In the one year of its existence, George Wolz's regiment lost seven men killed in action and sixty-five to disease—7 percent of its total strength—about average for Union regiments in the Civil War. Despite its deficiencies in equipment and the health of its men, six companies of the Third Cavalry received orders to march to Cassville, Missouri. It was time to take on the guerrillas.

Chapter 4

"Hard Service in the Way of Scouting"

"In Good Spirits Expecting to Have a Fight"

The guerrilla warfare that started with bridge burning and shootings into passing trains turned far deadlier in 1862. After Price retreated from Lexington to southwest Missouri and northwest Arkansas in the fall of 1861, many of his solders simply went home. There they found their families and homes threatened, if not already attacked and destroyed. Among the culprits were Kansas regiments—Jayhawkers—who swept into Missouri supposedly to protect Union interests in the area. Instead, they burned and looted homes and murdered men indiscriminately, Union and Secessionist alike. Not surprisingly, Secessionists struck back. The MSM, aided by regiments from other states such as Wisconsin, Iowa and Illinois, had its hands full.

The march from Chillicothe to Cassville was a hard one for the Third Cavalry. The commander of Company F, apparently supplied only with government horses, noted that they rode "over very rocky and mountainous country with but half rations for our horses of which we marched 150 miles bareback without bridles or halters except rope and hickory bark." The troopers commenced the first of many scouts in June. On a scout into Arkansas, Company F groused that its horses marched one hundred miles without horseshoes.

In the summer of 1862, rumors swirled about southwest Missouri that the Rebels were gathering once again for an invasion. Wolz's Company I was sent to Newtonia, on Oliver's Prairie, to set up an outpost there. A number of the roads connecting the lead mining areas along Centre Creek intersected at that little village. But on August 1, Wolz wrote to his brother just as his battalion, "in good Spirits Expecting to have to fight," was preparing to reinforce the Union troops at Cassville, "we Received Orders from General [Egbert B.] Brown to abandon Newtonia and Come to Springfield with all Possible Speed and to Burn our Bagage and Comisariy that we could not take." Wolz and the other troopers left at sundown and marched until 2:00 p.m. the next day, accompanied by 2,500 refugees, including women and children, making the column about seven miles long. They started the next night at 9:00 p.m. and did not stop until 10:00 a.m. Sunday morning. The men were too tired to eat. They just wanted to find some shade and sleep.

Their first big fight came the next Saturday evening. Troops from the First Missouri Volunteer Cavalry called for help when they were attacked by a superior force at Newtonia. Another cavalry detachment from Springfield relieved the beleaguered First Cavalry and drove the Confederates across the prairie to the north. The Third Cavalry took cover on the south side of Shoal Creek and awaited the fleeing Rebels. When they came into sight, Wolz boasted, "[we] poured a deadly fire into their Ranks which threw them into confusion and caused them to turn back." Caught between the pursing troops from Newtonia and the Federals blocking their way across the creek, the Confederates broke and ran. As for the "guerrilla Bands that [are] Prowling through this country almost all time and every Place," Wolz wrote, "that game is almost Plaid out…for there is strict orders against taking any more Prisoners that is found in arms or bush Whackers But to leave them on the ground we found them on."

The Third Cavalry camped in early November at Springfield, where it prepared to go into winter quarters. Wolz wrote home about the pretty girls he met in town and repeatedly requested more letters from his family. Back home in Grundy County, the soldiers' fathers, mothers, brothers and sisters also anxiously awaited news from their loved ones. The triweekly stage from Chillicothe brought letters and newspapers with news of the war. Its arrival, county historian James Everitt Ford wrote, was "the signal for a crowd to gather and listen while the address on each letter and paper was called out by the worthy postmistress, Mrs. Collier." The gathering then "adjourned to some convenient fence corner" to hear the newspapers read aloud by Mr. A.K. Sykes.

In the eleven months that George Wolz served in the Third Cavalry MSM, it experienced relatively little actual fighting compared to some

Although likely taken in the Eastern Theater, this photograph shows a typical cavalryman and his horse in 1862. Most soldiers in the MSM supplied their own horses, for which they were paid an additional forty cents per day for the "risk and use" of the animal. If their horses were killed in combat, the government reimbursed them for the appraised value, usually ranging from $80 to $100. George Wolz lost two horses in combat. *Library of Congress.*

other Missouri State Militia regiments. But it did see, as regimental surgeon Dr. Aurelius Bartlett noted, "a good deal of hardship and suffering, as the command…was required to do much hard service in the way of scouting."

"On They Came, Like a Tornado"

Milton Burch was thirty-nine when the war began. He enlisted in an Illinois infantry regiment during the Mexican-American War. Afterward, he moved to Buffalo, Dallas County, Missouri. Burch enrolled in the

Private John Durnell, from Dallas County, was mustered into Company A, Fourteenth Cavalry MSM, at Bennett's Mill, now Bennett Springs. He was wounded on August 4, 1862, in a dawn attack on guerrillas near Forsyth. Durnell was left with a Union family and later moved to Mount Vernon, where he died on August 19. *Wilson's Creek National Battlefield.*

Dallas County Home Guard and was elected second lieutenant. When the Home Guards were disbanded, Burch joined and helped recruit the Fourteenth Cavalry MSM. Among his recruits was John Durnell (also spelled "Durnil" in the official records), who joined Company A at Bennett's Mill (now Bennett's Spring) in January 1862.

Over the next few months, the Fourteenth Cavalry operated out of its base in Springfield, scouting and guarding paymasters and provision trains. Company A suffered a few casualties that spring: Sergeant John Butcher was wounded on a scout, and Sergeant William Potter was severely wounded when his seven-man patrol was attacked in Lawrence County by twenty-five guerrillas. On March 26, Lieutenant Abraham Worley led twenty-eight men from Sarcoxie up Centre Creek for eight miles. He captured a Confederate lieutenant colonel, a lieutenant and several privates.

Burch and Durnell's first significant action did not turn out so well. On May 30, about two hundred men from the Fourteenth Cavalry, including

Company A, marched from Mount Vernon to Neosho under the command of Colonel John M. Richardson. They camped on a flat area northwest of town, at the foot of a hill and only sixty yards from dense brush. Richardson and Burch posted parties of pickets on all of the roads leading through the area but failed to post any on the hill. The next morning, at about 8:00 a.m., four hundred men from Stand Watie's Cherokee Regiment and Colonel John Coffee's command attacked the Federal camp. Company A formed a line of battle and fired three rounds into the charging enemy. At that point, Richardson was wounded. A number of civilian refugees who had followed the militia in the hope of being restored to their homes began to flee. Richardson had sent all of his senior officers out of camp earlier that morning on other tasks. There was no one left to rally the troops. Within ten minutes, the entire force had melted away. The Confederates captured arms, ammunition, wagons, two flags and other equipment.

Burch's next foray was much more successful. In late July, he was in command of eighty men at Ozark, a few miles south of Springfield. He received word that Confederates under Colonel Robert Lawther were approaching to attack the post. On the night of August 1, Burch withdrew his men from the camp and hid them in the woods. The plan was to open fire after the Rebels charged into the camp firing their revolvers into the empty tents. Burch reported that the ruse worked perfectly:

> *Scarcely were these arrangements made when the pickets on the east commenced firing and rushed in, followed by the enemy, who poured out of the dark woods and thundered down upon our camp yelling like devils, and firing at our tents. On they came, like a tornado, striking our strong picket ropes, overturning some of their horses, and throwing the balance into disorder. Then was our time. The order to fire was given on the left, and as the guns roared out the men set up the most deafening yells. The enemy quickly fled on all directions.*

Two of Burch's men were wounded; the enemy lost nine wounded, three of them mortally. The next day, Burch was sent south to Forsyth to determine whether the Rebels were still in the area. He led eighty men composed of detachments from all of the companies of the Fourteenth Cavalry. Six of them came from Company A, including John Durnell.

With the assistance of local guides, Burch approached Lawther's camp at daybreak on August 4. Suddenly, they came upon the Confederate pickets, but these men did not give the alarm, looking at the Union cavalrymen "with astonishment, as if they did not know what our appearance meant." The pickets fled, and some of Burch's men charged into the enemy camp firing their revolvers. The remainder of Burch's men charged on foot. The enemy was caught in total surprise. The Rebels retreated to a nearby cornfield and "returned quite a spirited fire," mostly with shotguns. Private Mark Evans was hit with buckshot in the chin but was not seriously hurt. Sergeant John Baxter was hit full in the chest with a load of buckshot but was not hurt at all, as the shot did not even enter the flesh. But John Durnell was not so lucky. He was seriously wounded. Burch left him in the care of a Union citizen. Durnell lingered on but died on August 19 at Mount Vernon.

Chapter 5

"Continuously in the Saddle, Day and Night"

"It Will Be Nothing but Slaughter in the Thick Brush"

Thirteen-year-old William Caton desperately wanted to be a cavalryman like his father, Aaron, a tailor, who at age forty enlisted in Company E, Second Missouri Volunteer Cavalry in Chillicothe along with seventy other Livingston County men in September 1861. According to family lore, William asked and was refused at least six times, probably because he was far underage.

If George Wolz spent most of 1862 in scouting and patrols rather than combat, Aaron Caton spent that year in a series of hard fights with guerrillas.

Colonel Lewis Merrill was proud of his Second Missouri Volunteer Cavalry, dubbed "Merrill's Horse" by General Frémont. He touted it as the best-trained cavalry in Missouri, and it likely was. At a time when enlistments were lagging in Missouri, Merrill signed up eight hundred men in less than a month. Three companies were raised in north Missouri, Companies D, E and F; four companies were recruited in Michigan, Companies A, B, H and I; and three companies enlisted at Cincinnati, Companies C, G and K. Merrill had been a lieutenant in the regular cavalry and, later, the United States Dragoons. Thus, unlike most Missouri cavalry officers in both the volunteers and the state militia, Merrill had actual experience as a cavalryman. When his regiment was gathered at Benton Barracks in St. Louis, he immediately

Lewis Merrill was a regular army officer in the dragoons before the war. He recruited, organized and trained the Second Missouri Volunteer Cavalry, dubbed "Merrill's Horse" by Frémont. Merrill commanded a district in north Missouri and was not in direct command of his regiment in its 1862 actions. After the war, Merrill was assigned to the Seventh United States Cavalry and broke up Ku Klux Klan activities in South Carolina and Louisiana. *Library of Congress*.

This soldier from Company B of an unidentified regiment has the type of weapons carried by the Second Missouri Cavalry (Merrill's Horse) in 1862: a saber, Colt revolver and a Hall carbine. The side lever on the carbine opened the breech at the top for loading, but it leaked smoke into the shooter's face. The image is reversed because it is a direct positive—made directly from the camera, like a negative. *Library of Congress.*

instituted a regimen of military instruction and drill and worked his charges hard.

In January, three companies of Merrill's Horse (including Aaron Caton's Company E) participated in an attack on Confederate recruits gathered by Colonel John Poindexter near Silver Creek in Howard County, just across the county line from the railroad at Renick. Major Charles Hunt led his men, armed with Hall carbines, to the edge of the camp to provide a covering fire for the remainder of the force to charge with sabers and revolvers. Hunt drove in the enemy's pickets and rushed the entrance of the Rebel camp, but they were met with a volley that downed several men. After a brisk forty-minute battle in an area of ravines, thick underbrush and timber, the Rebels fled, leaving horses, guns and camp equipment behind. The Federals tried to pursue, but darkness fell and a heavy fog made it impossible.

The Union force lost six men killed and nineteen wounded but succeeded in capturing 160 horses, sixty wagons, 105 tents, eighty kegs of powder and two hundred rifles and shotguns. Twenty-five-year-old Alexander Keith, a farmer who had enlisted at Chillicothe in Company E along with Aaron Caton, was killed. Thomas Moore was wounded severely in the thigh. Henry Reading was luckier—his wounds in the right knee and left elbow were not severe. Jacob King, Company B, was shot in the head and died a few days later.

Merrill set up his headquarters on the campus of the University of Missouri in Columbia. Two companies each were stationed at Columbia, Fayette, Glasgow, Huntsville and Sturgeon. Samuel Baird, Company H, recalled that they were "almost continuously in the saddle, day and night, scouting for bushwhackers, for the county was full of them."

The Union troops in southwestern and southeastern Missouri principally contended with bands of guerrillas that would venture across the border from Arkansas for a few days to strike at wagon trains, patrols or isolated civilians. But in northeastern Missouri, the summer of 1862 saw a major push by the Confederate army to tap what Price believed was a large pool of Secessionist men eager to join the fight against the "invading" Federal forces.

Several Confederate officers, most notably Colonels Joseph Porter and John Poindexter, returned to Missouri to recruit. Although their primary job was recruiting, they often attacked towns, robbed and killed civilians and ambushed Federal troops in a manner indistinguishable from guerrillas, who lacked any such official trappings.

In mid-June, Porter crisscrossed Lewis and Marion Counties, carrying out sporadic attacks, then headed north into Schuyler County. The Second and Eleventh Cavalry MSM caught him in a running battle at Cherry Grove, near the Iowa line. They claimed to have killed twelve of Porter's men and wounded another twenty.

In the meantime, Major John Y. Clopper, with about 320 men from Companies A, C, E, F, H and I, set out to join the pursuit of Porter. They marched thirty-five to forty miles per day, with only the rations they could carry, through six days of continuous and drenching rain.

Porter arrived in Memphis, Scotland County, with 250 men and captured it with little trouble. The Rebels herded all of the men of military age into the courthouse and proceeded to steal what they wanted from the town's stores. Before leaving town, some of Porter's men hanged Dr. William Aylward, a prominent Union sympathizer.

Porter lingered in southwestern Scotland County for nearly a week. On July 18, Major Clopper, accompanied by a detachment from the Eleventh Cavalry MSM, found him there. The Federals rode into a trap carefully set by Porter. He left a few men on the bridge over the Middle Fabius River pretending that they were tearing it up. When Clopper's advance appeared, the Rebels fled. Porter stationed the bulk of his force a short distance up the road at Vassar Hill. The unsuspecting cavalry charged into the ambush, where many were gunned down by musket and shotgun fire. Porter withdrew to another, even better position. Twice more the Union cavalry charged up the road on their horses, and twice more they were met with a devastating hail of gunfire. After the third charge, Lieutenant George Rowell, temporarily in command of Company H, started to dismount his men to fight on foot. Major Clopper rode up and ordered another charge. "Major, for God's sake," Rowell protested, "don't order these mounted companies in there again; it will be nothing but slaughter in the thick brush." But Clopper ignored him. The cavalrymen charged and were repulsed three more times over a period of three hours. By the time Porter left the area for good, Clopper had suffered twenty-four killed and fifty-nine wounded—ten killed and thirty-five wounded from his regiment and the balance from the Eleventh Cavalry. Porter's losses were much less: six killed, three mortally wounded and ten wounded. Although Clopper portrayed the action as a smashing victory, with the enemy "whipped and in full flight," in fact it was his men who were beaten and who had to rest from the exhaustion of forced marches over bad roads in "constant rainy weather."

Porter moved south, apparently attempting to get his recruits across the Missouri River and into Arkansas. By July 25, Porter had reached Brown's Spring, on Auxvasse Creek in northern Callaway County. There he was joined by 140 guerrillas from Montgomery and Boone Counties, giving him about 350 men under his command.

William Caton was not the only underage Missourian who sought to join the fight against the Rebels. Ludwick St. John convinced his father to sign off on his son's enlistment at the reported age of seventeen—he was actually only fourteen. St. John joined Company A, Ninth Cavalry MSM, a regiment raised by Odon Guitar, a prominent lawyer, slaveholder and conservative Unionist from Columbia.

St. John's Company A and Company B were at Jefferson City when they got word that Porter had moved south. At 10:00 p.m. on July 27, Guitar crossed the river into Callaway County and marched all night to Brown Springs. Guitar was joined by one hundred men from Companies G and K of Merrill's Horse, led by Lieutenant Colonel William Shaffer. But when they arrived at Brown Springs, Porter was gone. He had decided to move to a better position to await the advance of the Union force. He deliberately left a well-marked trail along Auxvasse Creek in the hopes that the Federals would fall into another ambush as they had at Vassar Hill. The next day, July 28, Porter's men concealed themselves in the underbrush about one mile

Odon Guitar. Guitar, a successful lawyer in Columbia, raised the Ninth Cavalry MSM in central Missouri. He led a regiment in the Battle of Moore's Mill, defeating Confederate recruiter Joseph Porter. Later, he ruthlessly pursued Confederate recruiter John Poindexter through central Missouri, inflicting disastrous defeats at Switzler's Mill, Little Compton Ferry, and on the Muscle Fork of the Chariton River. *State Historical Society of Missouri.*

south of Moore's Mill and about one mile west of Auxvasse Creek (near present-day Calwood), waiting for the Federals to advance.

Guitar's men proceeded down the west side of Auxvasse Creek, while Shaffer's crossed it and rode down the east bank. At about 1:00 p.m., Guitar's advance stumbled into Porter's trap. Two volleys crashed into them. The Federals dismounted and returned the fire with a volley of their own. The remainder of Guitar's force came up, including two cannons, and deployed. In the brutal, airless July heat of mid-Missouri, the most the cavalrymen could see was occasional flashes from the muskets or shotguns through the smoke from the black powder that hung in clouds over the thick underbrush.

As the lines seesawed back and forth, fighting over the cannons, Shaffer arrived from the other side of the creek. Dismounted, Company G went to the right, part of Company K to the left and the remainder in reserve. In the rush to take its position, Company K was exposed to a raking musket and shotgun fire. Lieutenant Joseph Meyers was riddled with musket balls and buckshot and died shortly after the battle.

The timely intervention by Merrill's Horse staved off the Rebel advance. The forces settled back into a desultory gunfight that lasted another three hours before Porter, his ammunition nearly exhausted, pulled back and retreated. The Union troops, equally exhausted by the heat and lack of food, did not pursue.

The Battle of Moore's Mill resulted in Union losses of 20 dead and 55 wounded, including 6 killed and 11 wounded from Merrill's Horse. Confederate losses were 60 dead and 120 wounded.

Unable to get past Union troops to the Missouri River, Porter headed north again, attacking Paris and Newark along the way. By the time he reached Kirksville on August 3, Porter's strength had grown exponentially, to nearly two thousand men, but only half of them were armed.

Lieutenant Colonel Shaffer trailed Porter from the Moore's Mill battlefield. He joined a mixed force of seven hundred MSM cavalry, Iowa infantry and a section of the Third Indiana Battery, all commanded by Colonel John McNeil of the Second Cavalry MSM. Porter remained just out of their grasp, but "the militia," one of Porter's men wrote, "was crowding us on every side." McNeil pushed his men hard through "a most difficult country, following [Porter's] devious and eccentric windings through brake and bottom and across fields, where often no wheel had ever turned before." The Rebels destroyed bridges and felled trees to block fords, but the Federals pushed on.

On the morning of August 6, McNeil's forces approached Kirksville. The Confederates warned the townsfolk to leave and occupied the houses, the courthouse and the Cumberland Academy. McNeil sent Merrill's Horse to the right wing, along with detachments from the Second and Eleventh Cavalry MSM and the Indiana artillery. The Iowa infantry and the First Cavalry MSM were the left wing.

From the outskirts of town, the only Rebel soldier who could be seen was in the cupola of the courthouse. He was soon killed by a well-placed shot from a Sharps rifle fired by Colonel McNeil's "colored man Jim…who did splendid work throughout the afternoon. Whenever a rebel showed his head at long range Jim was almost certain to get him."

With Porter's men hidden in town, McNeil called for a reconnaissance party to discover their exact whereabouts. Shaffer ordered Second Lieutenant John Coudrey of Company A, Merrill's Horse, to take eight men to charge

Professor Allen Towne of the State Normal School (now Truman State University) drew this picture of the Battle of Kirksville with the assistance of veterans. Colonel (later General) John McNeil is on horseback near the Cumberland Academy on the right of the picture. In the left center is the courthouse. McNeil's "colored man Jim" shot a Rebel soldier in the cupola at long range with his Sharps rifle to start the engagement. *Wilson's Creek National Battlefield.*

through the town. Coudrey's squad approached the northeast corner of the square, where it was met with a fusillade from the Confederates in the buildings. Coudrey rode around the square, came out on the southwest corner and made a dash back to Union lines. Two of his men were mortally wounded, three others were wounded and five of their horses were killed. But the Rebel position was revealed.

McNeil directed the artillery to open fire, making many of Porter's new recruits "very nervous, they never before having heard anything of the kind." Company C, Merrill's Horse, along with the other Federal troops dismounted and seized the first line of houses and sheds on the northeast side of town. Gradually, the Union soldiers cleared the town in a bitter house-to-house battle. Finally, the Rebels broke ranks and took to the brush. Major Clopper led the pursuit to the Chariton River, but the dense brush between Kirksville and the river made the hunt difficult. In addition, both the men and the horses were broken down. Some had been in the saddle for thirty-two days, and none had eaten anything for the last two days.

John McNeil. McNeil was colonel of the Second Cavalry MSM, 1861–63. He was promoted to brigadier general despite his involvement in the execution of Confederates at Palmyra that led to an international furor. As a brigade commander, he fought at Jefferson City, Independence and Big Blue during Price's invasion of 1864. *Library of Congress*.

McNeil reported that he lost five killed and thirty-two wounded, including four killed and nine wounded from Merrill's Horse. Porter's losses are uncertain, but he lost at least one hundred dead and two hundred wounded. McNeil noted that they captured forty-seven prisoners, including fifteen who had been captured before and paroled on the promise, punishable by death, that they would not take up arms again. "I enforced the penalty of the bond by ordering them shot...Disposed that an evidence of clemency and mercy of the country toward the erring and misguided should go hand-in-hand with unrelenting justice, I discharged on parole all the prisoners who had not violated parole and who were in arms for the first time against their country and Government."

John Poindexter, undeterred by his defeat at Silver Creek, resumed recruiting duty in Missouri in the summer, but with a much lower profile—certainly much lower than Porter's. Between June and August, Poindexter raised about 1,100 troops. Nonetheless, his presence became known to Union troops. Colonel Guitar, fresh from the fight at Moore's Mill—with 550 men, including 100 under Major Hunt from Merrill's Horse and three companies from the Seventh Cavalry MSM under Lieutenant Colonel Thomas Crittenden—doggedly pursued Poindexter for seven days. He attacked the Confederates at Switzler's Mill and Little Compton Ferry and on the Muscle Fork of the Chariton River. By the time of the last battle, Poindexter's strength had dropped to 400 men. Guitar claimed to have killed, wounded or drowned 150 of his men and to have captured 100. Company D of the Seventh Cavalry reported that it killed 30 Rebels with a single volley at Compton's Ferry while they were attempting to cross the Grand River in a ferryboat.

Poindexter led the remnants of his command to Utica, southwest of Chillicothe, but ran into a force led by Brigadier General Benjamin Loan ordered from St. Joseph to join in the pursuit. The next day, Guitar's men caught him again, this time at Yellow Creek in Chariton County. Poindexter was thoroughly beaten.

Other recruiters, led by Captain Robert Austin, were attempting to join Poindexter. Stranded south of the Missouri River, they came upon the steamer *War Eagle* in the Missouri River bottoms of Saline County. A few shots stopped the vessel. The Rebels boarded it and compelled the master to ferry them to the north bank of the river. After commandeering food and other supplies, Austin's men continued their journey north. A few days later, however, a patrol from the Fifth Cavalry MSM discovered Austin's camp. The Federals recaptured the supplies taken from the *War Eagle* and killed

War Eagle. In 1861, Rebels transported guns and ammunition captured at the Liberty Arsenal to St. Joseph on this vessel, sealed in whiskey barrels and tobacco crates. Guerrillas briefly captured it in July 1862. In July 1864, Anderson's men fired thirty shots into the boat from Rocheport. *Herman Pott Collection, St. Louis Mercantile Library at the University of Missouri–St. Louis.*

thirty-six Confederates in a running fight that ended three days later on the banks of the Grand River. The Rebels scattered and fled in all directions.

After a summer of hard riding and hard fighting by several detachments, Merrill's Horse reassembled in Columbia. That fall, it continued scouting, and late in the year, it began preparing winter quarters. Colonel Merrill did not let the men rest; rather, under his direct supervision, the regiment trained in the evolutions of the cavalry regiment as set forth in Philip St. George Cooke's manual of tactics.

In October 1862, Merrill, after being besieged by young William Caton, finally relented and said that he would be allowed to enlist if he learned to play the bugle that day. No doubt aided by a bugler from the regiment, Caton learned to play Taps. He enlisted in his father's company,

Opposite: This is the cover for sheet music of the song "The Merrill Horse or the Guerrillas Conquered," published in 1863. In florid lyrics, the composer praised the regiment for confronting the "guerrilla chief monster entrench'd in his den" at Silver Creek and for their "death stroke to Porter" at the Battle of Kirksville, where "hundreds of guerrillas licked dust." *Library of Congress*.

Above: This unidentified soldier is wearing the uniform of a bugler, similar to the one worn by William Caton of Company E, Second Missouri Volunteer Cavalry ("Merrill's Horse"). Because cavalry commands were given by the company's buglers, they were required to wear stripes (and sometimes ride distinctively colored horses) so that the commander could find them in the heat of battle. *Library of Congress*.

Company E, on October 1, 1862, after Aaron, with a wink to regulations, gave his written consent, certifying that his son was seventeen. William served the rest of the war.

"A DEMON IN BATTLE...THIS INFAMOUS SCOUNDREL"

While Merrill's Horse and Guitar's Ninth Cavalry MSM were primarily fighting Confederate recruiters in central and northeastern Missouri, Federals troops in western Missouri had to deal with both recruiters and bands of guerrillas. The guerrillas sometimes cooperated with the recruiters but more often operated on their own. The latter, many of whom were soldiers returning home from Price's army, initially organized to protect their families and homes from jayhawker depredations. Their membership was fluid. At any one time, the guerrillas might muster anywhere from a handful of men to one hundred or more. Any man who could gather men to follow him could be a guerrilla leader.

Although there were numerous guerrilla leaders active in western Missouri, the best known was William Quantrill. Quantrill was born in Canal Dover, Ohio, in 1837. In 1857, he moved to Kansas. He fought at Wilson's Creek and Lexington. He left the army on its retreat from Lexington and returned to Jackson County. By Christmas, he had organized his own band of guerrillas. Quantrill was a charismatic and fearless leader. Years after the war, Frank James still marveled at meeting him. "I will never forget the first time I saw Quantrill. He was nearly six feet in height, rather thin, his hair and mustache was sandy and he was full of life and a jolly fellow. He had none of the air of bravado or the desperado about him, [but] he was a demon in battle."

Quantrill's raids into Kansas in early 1862 brought him national attention. The public's fascination with him led many, including Federal officers, to blame him for any guerrilla attack in western Missouri whether he or his men were involved or not. He also escaped several close calls in 1862 that added to his reputation. Of course, Quantrill was also the leader of the murderous raid on Lawrence, Kansas, in 1863 that cemented his notoriety during the Civil War as well as today.

On January 29, Quantrill set up an ambush near Blue Springs. With eighteen men, he caught a Seventh Missouri Infantry patrol in a defile leading

Northwest Missouri during the Civil War. Western Missouri was plagued by guerrillas led by William Quantrill, Bill Anderson and George Todd. The rugged Sni hills in eastern Jackson County and western Lafayette County were favorite hideouts. Jackson, Cass, Bates and northern Vernon Counties were cleared of civilians by Order No. 11 in 1863, and they became known as the Burnt District. *Map by Colter Sikora.*

to a crossing of the Little Blue River. In the ensuing gun battle, the Federals claimed that they killed two guerrillas; the guerrillas claimed that they captured all of the Union troops and paroled them. The patrol leader later wrote, "I have seen this infamous scoundrel rob mails, steal the coaches and horses, and commit similar outrages upon society even within sight of this city. Mounted on the best horses of the country, he has defied pursuit, making his camp in the [river bottoms], and roving over a circuit of 30 miles."

On March 22, Quantrill captured and shot a lone Union sergeant standing guard at the bridge over the Little Blue River. The Union commander ordered a pursuit. On a tip, Union soldiers went to the home of David Tate. They were surprised to find Quantrill himself hiding in the Tate house. The Federals called for him to surrender or they would set the place on fire. They were met with a volley from the guerrillas. When they attempted to fire the house, Private William Wills took a Minié ball in the right arm and buckshot to his groin and abdomen. He died later. The second attempt to set the house on fire succeeded, but Quantrill and most of his men escaped by prying off the weatherboarding at the rear of the house and fleeing into the woods. Two were killed before they reached the woods; five died in the fire.

Four days later, Quantrill and two hundred men charged into Warrensburg to attack the post there manned by Major Emory Foster and sixty men of the Seventh Cavalry MSM. Foster, however, stationed his men in the brick county courthouse and surrounded it with a stockade. Quantrill lost nine dead and seventeen wounded. He made a brief effort to renew the fight the next day but soon melted back into the brush of Jackson County. He had learned a lesson that he would not forget.

On March 30, Quantrill's men rendezvoused at the Samuel Clark farm nineteen miles southeast of Independence. The Clark home was a double log house situated on a hill above the road. Captain Albert Peabody led thirty men from Company D, First Missouri Volunteer Cavalry, in a search of the area. As they passed the Clark place, the guerrillas opened fire. Peabody left a few men to tend to the horses and led the rest on foot to attack the log cabin. They fired at the windows and doors for over an hour and a half. The guerrillas returned the fire through loopholes made by knocking out the plaster between the logs. More guerrillas joined the fight from their nearby camp. Finally, Peabody was reinforced by thirty-five men led by Lieutenant William White. They charged the Clark house and drove the Rebels out. As usual, the guerrillas faded into the brush, where they could not be effectively chased. Peabody lost three wounded; he claimed that six guerrillas were killed and twenty of their horses were captured. In retaliation for the harboring of the guerrillas, Peabody burned the Clark house and all of its outbuildings. The next day, a Federal patrol of fifty men from the Boonville Battalion MSM jumped Quantrill's men at Ball's Ford on Sni-A-Bar Creek. After briefly exchanging revolver fire, Quantrill once again took to the brush to evade the Union troops.

Quantrill escaped disaster for the third time in mid-April. On April 14, his men were camped at the Lowe house, twelve miles southwest of Independence. Lieutenant George Nash of the First Missouri Volunteer Cavalry and thirty men had been tracking the guerrillas for five days. A heavy thunderstorm pelted the Union troopers until 4:00 a.m., but this provided them cover as they crept into position. At daybreak, they charged the farmhouse, catching the Rebels completely by surprise. Quantrill and his fled the into the woods about one hundred yards away, leaving behind four dead, four wounded, five prisoners and nearly all of the horses, weapons and coats. (Nash was court-martialed in the summer of 1862 for murder of a civilian; he ran away during the trial and was dishonorably discharged. Nash was captured in Virginia and sent to Gratiot Prison in St. Louis until he was paroled in 1863.)

These setbacks did not deter Quantrill or other guerrillas from continued attacks on Federal troops and especially on mail carriers and steamboats. On April 18, the *Kansas City Journal* noted that no mail had reached that town for three weeks. Mail carriers refused to travel in western Missouri without a military escort. But such escort duty was extremely dangerous—as historian Richard Brownlee pointed out, it merely provided more targets for the guerrillas. Lieutenant Colonel James Buel of the Seventh Missouri Volunteer Cavalry reached what he hoped was at least a temporary solution by ordering that the mail be carried by Secessionists because he was "unwilling that any more of my men shall be murdered by escorting this mail."

The skirmishes became increasingly brutal as the year wore on. On June 16, a patrol of eighteen men from Company G, Seventh Cavalry MSM, was ambushed by guerrillas nine miles west of Warrensburg. The encounter developed into a running fight until the patrol was surrounded by nearly one hundred guerrillas. They managed to send a runner to town for reinforcements, which immediately mounted up and headed west. The guerrillas, however, got away. The patrol had left three wounded men in the brush. The rescue party found the bodies of two of them, riddled with revolver balls and horribly mutilated. The third man, Corporal Thomas Holston, was safe. He had crawled six miles through the brush to escape the enemy. After a short hospital stay, he returned to duty the next month.

Holston's luck did not hold, though, as he drowned on October 6, 1864, according to his service record, "attempting to swim the Osage River to escape the enemy" during the fighting around Jefferson City.

On July 8, word came to Major James Gower of the First Iowa Cavalry that Quantrill and about two hundred of his men were camped on Sugar Creek in southeastern Cass County. He sent a detachment of ninety men out that night at 11:00 p.m. At daylight, the Iowans charged the campsite but were driven off after receiving several volleys. Gower sent word to Union troops near Butler and Warrensburg, asking that they converge the next day on the Lotspeich farm, one mile west of Quantrill's position. Gower's sixty-five men were met by another sixty-five from the First Iowa's detachment at Butler; by sixty-five men from the Seventh Missouri Volunteer Cavalry, who had answered the call of "boots and saddles" at 3:00 a.m. at their camp four miles west of Kingsville; and by sixty-one men from the First Missouri Volunteer Cavalry led by Captain Miles Kehoe. But their quarry had left the prior afternoon.

Kehoe reported that he found Gower's command feeding the horses and eating breakfast. Rather than fall farther behind, Kehoe said that he would immediately start after the bushwhackers. He located their trail on Big Creek and sent word back. Gower's men hustled northeastward and struck Big Creek near Rose Hill and then began to follow it northwestward. He caught up with Kehoe at the Hornsby farm, three miles west of Pleasant Hill. At this point, the Federal officers' stories diverge. Kehoe claimed that the plan was to leave at daybreak; his men were ready to go at the appointed time, but Gower's were not. Gower alleged that Kehoe disobeyed a direct order and started after Quantrill on his own, presumably to take the lion's share of glory by defeating the guerrillas before the rest of the Union troops could arrive. If that was Kehoe's intent, it did not work out that way.

Kehoe came upon Quantrill at the Sears farm, six miles west of Pleasant Hill. There he saw a man, guerrilla William Gregg, in apparent distressed surprise. The First Missouri charged down the lane toward the farmhouse. Suddenly, they were met by gunfire from all sides. The first six men—Corporals Elijah White and George Darkin and Privates Richard Masters, William Trumpee, G.H. Walker and William Ritcher—fell dead. Nine more were wounded, including Captain Kehoe, who took a round to the shoulder. The guerrillas stripped the bodies of their weapons. Once out of range, Kehoe dismounted the rest of his men. They returned fire, driving the guerrillas from the farm into a ravine, five to seven feet deep and forty to sixty feet wide, surrounded by brush. Upon arriving, Gower's men charged but were beaten back. Captain William Martin led his men to the edge of the ravine, holding their fire until only fifteen feet away from the Rebels. They jumped down the side and drove the guerrillas out to the other side.

In the confusion of the next hour and a half, Quantrill's men and the Union cavalry blasted away at each other with carbines, revolvers, shotguns and rifles—sometimes not more than fifty feet distant. Despite the fierceness of the fight, the close quarters and the amount of ammunition expended, the Federals lost only four more men killed, three from the First Iowa (George Collins, James Beecroft and Suel Dodge) and one from the Seventh Missouri (Samuel Nicholas). Quantrill's losses are not known, but Gower claimed that his men killed fourteen and wounded at least another eighteen. Evidently, the dense brush and the poor marksmanship of both sides kept the casualties in what accounts from both sides characterized as a "hand-to-hand" fight to a relative minimum. Quantrill was wounded in the thigh. He lost his horse and saddle. The Federals found a useful document in his personal effects: two copies of a muster roll listing ninety-three men as members of his band.

Quantrill's success in disrupting normal activities in Jackson, Cass, Johnson and Lafayette Counties infuriated the district commander, Brigadier General James ("Old Bottle Nose") Totten. He issued a special order condemning the guerrillas and those helping them. He grumbled that the whole area had been reduced to a state of anarchy by the "well-known and desperate leader of these outlaws by the name of Quantrill." Totten threatened that all such persons found in arms "will be shot down by the military on the spot when found perpetrating their foul acts." Those assisting them would be subject to being tried by a military commission.

Totten's fulminations had little success in curbing guerrilla activities. Quantrill and other guerrillas found perfect hideouts in the impenetrable thickets along the ravines, creeks and rivers of western Missouri. They received not only food and clothing from sympathetic civilians—frequently family members of the gang—but also information concerning the whereabouts and movements of the Union forces. Quantrill learned from the mistakes in the summer of 1862 that nearly got him killed: they needed to post better security, avoid pitched battles with Union troops and avoid attacks on fortified positions such as the brick courthouses found in the county seats. And if attacked, their best tactic was to scatter into the brush to rendezvous later at a predetermined spot. As Quantrill told one of his men, "scattered soldiers make a scattered trail. The regiment that has but one man to hunt can never find him." A Federal soldier complained, "They've all scattered but one man and there's no use following him, for he'll scatter like the rest of 'em."

Chapter 6

"Few Things Perplex Me More"

THE CANTANKEROUS BAZEL LAZEAR

Bazel Lazear was an ardent, but conservative, Unionist. A resident of the little village of Ashley, he joined the Pike County Home Guards in July 1861 as captain of Company B. When that unit was disbanded, he joined the Six Month Militia. That regiment was mustered out in January 1862, and Lazear joined the Twelfth Cavalry MSM as a major under the command of Colonel Albert Jackson.

Lazear never got along with his commanding officers. Indeed, there was even opposition to his appointment to the Twelfth Cavalry. His complaints were at least partly responsible for Jackson's removal, creating a controversy over Governor Gamble's authority to sack incompetent officers that eventually required the personal intervention of President Lincoln—yet another headache from Missouri that the president had to deal with. Lazear was transferred to the First Cavalry MSM in 1863, but he got along no better with his superior officers there. He carried on months-long disputes with his regimental and district commanders. To Lazear's satisfaction, both were court-martialed for their conduct during Sterling Price's invasion of Missouri in 1864. They were, however, both acquitted and restored to duty.

Lazear was initially assigned to command Companies A, C and D at Cape Girardeau. In July 1862, he assumed command of the post at Greenville. On July 16, Lazear was ordered away and left the post in command of Captain

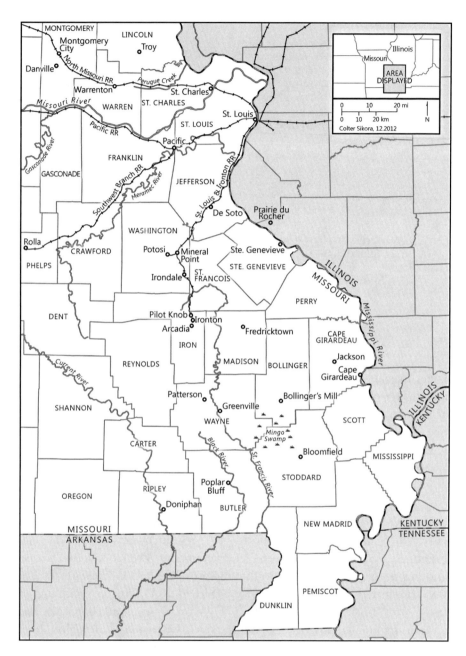

Southeast Missouri during the Civil War. The swamps and hills of southeast Missouri provided hiding places for guerrillas that Union troops found difficult to penetrate. This region saw merciless guerrilla warfare beginning in 1863. Pilot Knob was the scene of a pyrrhic Confederate victory in 1864. *Map by Colter Sikora.*

William Leeper of Company B. According to Colonel Jackson, Leeper had distinguished himself in an action in February when, with about twenty-five men of his company, he withstood an assault by Confederate colonel Jeff Thompson near Mingo Swamp. The remainder of the command broke and ran, but Leeper's men stood fast and prevented a pursuit by the enemy that would have made the defeat even more complete.

Leeper's Company B and Captain William Bangs's Company G camped in an orchard on top of a bluff east of the St. Francis River and about half a mile north of Greenville. Leeper's brother showed up on July 19 and reported that Timothy Reeves, a Confederate officer and guerrilla, was in the area. Despite this news, Leeper took no special precautions. He only posted pickets north and south of the camp, not to the more vulnerable east. All the company officers were absent except for Leeper and Lieutenant John Darnell from Company G. That same night, in the midst of a torrential downpour and thunderstorm, a number of men in Leeper's company got drunk.

In the early morning darkness of July 20, Reeves's men crept through the brush east of the camp to within a few yards of the orchard. Suddenly, they rushed forward, yelling and firing their weapons. The Federals were taken totally by surprise. The men up and sober were taking care of their horses when the attack began. They tried to get their rifles, but the confusion was too great. The bluecoats scattered. Most of them ran across the river. Assistant Surgeon Henry Douglas tried to rally some men from Company G, but Lieutenant Darnell refused to help. Finally, Sergeant Jesse Wicker volunteered to lead the men back. They fired a few rounds at the enemy but did little damage.

Leeper lost two men killed and five wounded. The Rebels took all of Company B's weapons, except for about thirty rifles, and stole Leeper's horse. The Twelfth's lieutenant colonel asked for reports from others who had been at Greenville. Douglas, Bangs and Leeper's own first lieutenant and first sergeant criticized Leeper for making the same kind of mistakes that Colonel Richardson made at Neosho: the camp was too near the woods, warnings of nearby guerrillas were ignored, the pickets were not properly posted and all of the senior officers were absent. Lieutenant Darnell was dismissed from the service for incompetency. Sergeant Wicker was promoted to first sergeant. Charges were preferred against Captain Leeper, but they went nowhere at that time. (He was finally removed for incompetence in 1864. Leeper seemed to have powerful friends in Washington after the war, for in 1891, the War Department reversed his dismissal.)

In late August, Major Lazear led 268 men from four companies of the Twelfth Cavalry from Patterson toward Greenville in search of what he told his wife was "a band of horse thieves" (they were actually guerrillas led by William Jeffers). He wished for more men, but many were sick from supplementing their rations with too many melons, peaches and green corn. After a few days on the march, they received word that Jeffers was camped on Crooked Creek about five miles southeast of Dallas. Leeper's Company B was riding down the creek in the advance when they were fired on by Confederates from behind a fence. Leeper's horse was shot from under him. Lazear later wrote to his wife with disgust that Leeper's entire company "wheeled, without firing a gun, and came running back through the lines of Company A, throwing them into confusion." The fleeing troopers rode through the next two companies, breaking up their line and creating a panic among them. After falling back for half a mile, Lazear was able to rally about twenty men and had them dismount behind another fence. Their fire stopped the Rebels, but the Federals were thoroughly defeated. They lost three killed and twenty wounded, not to mention twenty horses killed and wounded. Lazear and his horse, Button, were luckier, escaping without a scratch.

A State Governor Can Fill a Vacancy, but He Cannot Create It

If Lazear's military fortunes with the guerrillas were mixed, he was much more successful in his campaign to have Colonel Jackson removed as commander of the Twelfth Cavalry MSM. Complaints about Jackson reached headquarters in St. Louis, which dispatched an officer to investigate the situation. He found the grievances well founded and recommended that Jackson be removed for incompetence. Jackson protested and demanded a board of inquiry. The state militia adjutant general obliged and convened a panel in St. Louis. On September 10, 1862, the board found Jackson incompetent as a commander, and Governor Gamble vacated his commission.

Jackson may have been a poor soldier, but he was a persistent bureaucratic infighter. He immediately challenged the authority of a *state* militia board and the governor to revoke his commission. He was

Henry Halleck. In 1861, Halleck issued the first "no quarter" order against guerrillas caught burning railroad bridges. He and Governor Gamble squared off over the latter's authority to dismiss Missouri State Militia officers for incompetence. The issue was resolved by Lincoln, who declared that "few things perplex me more" than this kind of bureaucratic wrangling. Lincoln ordered that Gamble had the authority he sought, subject to final approval by the secretary of war. *Library of Congress.*

an officer of the Missouri State Militia, which was in *Federal*, not state, service. Therefore, he could only be removed by the federal government. He appealed to the War Department to reverse Governor Gamble's action.

In the meantime, Gamble wrote to General Henry Halleck (the former Union commander in Missouri and now the administrative commander in chief of the army) on a related matter. He asked about the nature of his authority over the Missouri State Militia, which was organized under the agreement with President Lincoln whereby the Federal government would equip and pay the men. Gamble asserted that, under the agreement, the MSM was still a state force, subject to his orders.

Halleck, a lawyer by training, replied in a characteristically detailed seven-page letter. He carefully parsed the terms of the agreement reached between Gamble and the president. He reviewed constitutional and statutory provisions governing the appointment of officers of the militia, concluding that Federal officers must be able to command state militia units. Any other arrangement would result in a "perfect state of military anarchy." Therefore, this interpretation must be the correct one.

Halleck sent another letter to Gamble upon receiving Colonel Jackson's appeal. He said that it was the position of the War Department that only the president or his designated officers had the "power to try, punish, or dismiss an officer of State militia in the service of the United States…No such power has been given to a Governor of a State over such troops…A State Governor can fill the vacancy so created, but he cannot himself create the vacancy." The agreement approved by Lincoln stipulated that the Missouri governor could appoint the officers of the MSM, but nowhere did it authorize him to remove them. Accordingly, Governor Gamble's dismissal of Albert Jackson was reversed as "without authority of law."

Halleck followed up his "official" reply with an "unofficial" letter to Gamble. He explained that his official letters were intended not only for Gamble but also "as a general answer to claims raised in other States in regard to command" of militias then being organized under the call of Congress for more troops. Halleck suggested that the Missouri agreement that Gamble relied on was ambiguous, perhaps deliberately so. As for the official letters, "The conclusions arrived at were those which I was directed to communicate to you. Perhaps they are right, and perhaps not."

General Halleck was a stickler for the niceties of the law, but in exchanging legal quiddities, he met his match in Hamilton Gamble. The governor had practiced law for more than thirty years and had been a judge of the Missouri Supreme Court (he had, in fact, voted in favor of Dred Scott on narrow technical grounds). Gamble pointed out that Halleck's first letter did not even answer the question asked. He bristled at the suggestion that the agreement with President Lincoln was ambiguous—Gamble was, after all, the author of the document. The provisions that Halleck singled out were inserted by an underling at the War Department after the president approved it. Gamble was "astonished…at the imprudent act of a subordinate," but he did not object because they did not, in his view, alter the meaning of the instrument.

Gamble nevertheless reluctantly acquiesced in the War Department's ruling, pending a resolution of the issue by the president. Colonel Jackson was reinstated to his command.

In the meantime, Lazear (newly promoted to lieutenant colonel) led an expedition from Patterson against Confederate colonel David Boone in Carter County. On the night of October 22, the Twelfth Cavalry surprised Boone in his camp. Three days later, Lazear's men caught up with Boone between the waters of Pike Creek and the Eleven Point River. They chased them all evening, killing eight and capturing eighteen. Colonel William Dewey led his Twenty-third Iowa Infantry and detachments of the First, Twenty-fourth and Twenty-fifth Missouri Infantry, with orders to meet Lazear's force at Pitman's Ferry on the Current River on the twenty-sixth. The combined forces were to attack about one thousand Rebels under John Burbridge. Dewey arrived at the ferry after a forced march. They skirmished briefly with the Confederates but were in no position to pursue them. Lazear received the orders too late to make the rendezvous. When the two forces finally joined, they chased the Rebels into Arkansas, but Burbridge escaped. However, General Davidson, the Union commander, viewed the actions as a success, praising the troops for behaving like veterans.

Despite Davidson's comments, Dewey criticized Lazear for his tardiness. Lazear, not one to suffer in silence, retorted that the Twenty-third Iowa behaved atrociously while operating in the area. The principal point of his letter, however, was to further charge Colonel Jackson with neglect of duty for his failure to protect Union civilians from the Iowans and to criticize him—nearly to the point of calling him a coward—for failing to assist other Union troops in actions against the enemy. Lazear complained of Jackson's "disgraceful" conduct and said that he could not serve in the same regiment with him. The letter was returned with instructions to put his charges into proper form. This he did with an even lengthier response that detailed numerous instances of Jackson's misconduct that ranged from incompetence in command to stealing an axe from one of the company officers.

The question of a state governor's right to remove militia officers—more precisely, Governor Gamble's right to remove militia officers under the 1862 agreement—finally reached President Lincoln in November. Gamble sought the assistance of Attorney General Edward Bates in getting Lincoln to intervene with the War Department. An exasperated Lincoln wrote to Bates, "Few things perplex me more than this question between Governor Gamble and the War Department." He took a practical view: the Missouri State Militia was of "mixed character." It was, in Lincoln's opinion, safer

These soldiers are (left to right) Private Henry Emme, Captain William Flentge, Private Dedrick Klingemann and Private August Klemme. This photograph is from a panorama of thirty-eight men from Company K, Fifth Missouri MSM, produced in 1865 at Rolla just before being mustered out. Emme and Klingemann served as company cooks, and Klemme was a regimental orderly. Flentge was a colleague of Bazel Lazear in the Twelfth Cavalry MSM before being reassigned. *Missouri History Museum.*

to decide the question only as it related to the Missouri militia, rather than by "deciding a general abstraction" that would only lead to further controversies with other governors. Lincoln said that allowing Gamble to vacate the officer's commissions and having the Secretary of War ratify the actions "ought to be satisfactory."

That was the final resolution, despite Gamble's further protests. On January 6, the War Department endorsed the power of Governor Gamble to remove officers "of that peculiar military force organized by him in Missouri," subject to confirmation by the department. Upon receipt of the order, Colonel Jackson at first turned over his regimental records to Lazear and "was at the point of leaving when he assumed command again issuing an order ordering [Lazear to be placed under] arrest." Lazear refused the order and put Jackson under guard. The next day, Jackson told some of the officers and men that he was taking a few days' leave. He added that Lazear was under arrest and that Captain William Flentge was taking command. Lazear called Jackson to his headquarters and sent him on his way, concluding that "I was only wasting time with a childish old man." Jackson did request leave from district headquarters to visit his seriously ill wife in Chicago, but his request was curtly refused because he "is now a private citizen and does not require a leave of absence."

Chapter 7

"An Immediate and Pressing Necessity"

"Bring Whatever Arms He May Have...and a Good Horse"

The explosion of guerrilla activity in the state in the early months of 1862—particularly the recruiting efforts of Porter and Poindexter—coupled with the demand for the regular volunteer forces of Missouri and other states to be sent to the other theaters to confront the principal Confederate armies, strained the Union anti-guerrilla effort. To offset these losses, General John Schofield suggested to Governor Gamble that he call out additional men to serve in a state-controlled and financed militia. Gamble agreed. He authorized Schofield to raise and order into service as many men as needed. Schofield duly issued General Order No. 19 on July 22, 1862, calling for every able-bodied man between the ages of eighteen and forty-five to report to the nearest military post to enroll in the militia. He was to bring "whatever arms he may have or can procure, and a good horse, if he has one." There he would be assigned to a company or regiment of the Enrolled Missouri Militia (EMM). (John Wolz, George's older brother, joined Company B, Thirtieth EMM, in Livingston County.)

The EMM was generally to be on active duty for not more than thirty days. The troops were to act as "minutemen" who would be called out in cases of emergency and mostly (but certainly not exclusively) to guard

John Schofield. Schofield was appointed commander of the Missouri State Militia in accordance with the Gamble-Lincoln agreement creating that force requiring the state militia to be commanded by a Federal officer. At Schofield's suggestion, Governor Gamble required all men between the ages of eighteen and forty-five to join the Enrolled Missouri Militia or declare themselves disloyal. Instead, many "took to the brush" to join Confederate forces or to hide from Federals enforcing the order. *Library of Congress.*

fixed installations such as key railroad bridges, towns and the like. When on active duty, the Federal government was to provide subsistence, but the EMM was also authorized to take what it needed from Southern sympathizers. The state, however, was responsible for the men's pay, a task that strained its already weak finances. The funds were obtained from several sources. Most of the money came from the issuance of defense warrants or bonds. These instruments were issued in sheets of small denominations as pay for the men. Derided as "Gamble shinplasters," the EMM soldiers could use them to pay their state taxes. They weren't worth much for any other purpose. Those enrolled as disloyal were assessed to help pay the EMM wages. Money also came from a levy of ten to thirty dollars that could be paid to be exempt from service. The latter source of funds was harshly criticized, especially by Radical Republicans, who complained not only that wealthier citizens could escape service altogether, but also that loyal men were paying for the defense of the loyal and disloyal. The exemption law was finally repealed in January 1864.

The EMM was even more indifferently armed than the MSM. The state and Federal government provided some weapons, but to the extent that these units had any arms at all, they were usually those brought from home. For example, of the three companies from the Forty-third Regiment at Tipton, just one had a rifle for every man. Only half of the soldiers in the other two companies were armed at all, and they had only double- or single-barreled shotguns. A fifty-five-man EMM company in Jefferson County had among them two old muskets, sixteen shotguns and five squirrel rifles.

Given the limited scope of its service, the government did not even supply uniforms for the EMM. Some officers received blue coats and regulation hats, but the men simply wore their civilian clothes. This presented a problem of identification for other Federal troops: were the armed men in the distance EMM or guerrillas? As a remedy, Federal commanders directed the EMM to wear white bands on their hats. Even this was not foolproof, for guerrillas would often adopt the same badge as a disguise—just as they would frequently wear captured blue coats.

By the late summer of 1862, Order No. 19 had produced an additional fifty-two thousand men, formed into seventy regiments, three battalions and fifty-eight independent companies. Of necessity, these units were untrained and were notoriously undisciplined. A distressing number of men took advantage of their newfound military authority to harass, or even rob or kill, neighbors against whom they bore grudges or whom they suspected or knew to be Southern sympathizers.

This bridge over Peruque Creek in St. Charles County was a strategic point on the North Missouri Railroad. Union troops built blockhouses to guard vital bridges in the event of raids. These men are from Company E, Twenty-seventh EMM, called out in October 1864. Captain Henry Denker is seated, reading. Note the white stripes on the hats to distinguish them from guerrillas because most EMM soldiers had no uniforms. *St. Charles County Historical Society.*

Some Union men were troubled by Order No. 19 because it was, in effect, conscription even before the Federal government began conscription, a practice that had previously been prohibited. Governor Gamble and General Schofield failed to consult higher authorities before taking this drastic step. The latter informed Washington that he suggested the measure to Gamble because the level of guerrilla violence reached the point that it was an "immediate and pressing necessity...to call at once all of the militia of the State" into service. It had the additional benefit of allowing Schofield to release regular volunteer units for service in other theaters, which repeatedly called for more troops.

But the most controversial provision of the decree was the clarifying Order No. 24, which provided that *disloyal* men report to the nearest military post to register as such. They were to surrender their arms and return to their homes and businesses, where—supposedly—they would not be disturbed if they "continue[d] quietly attending to their ordinary and legitimate business and in no way [gave] aid or comfort to the enemy." Some Federal commanders anticipated, correctly, that the forced reporting of disloyalty would "create as stampede of secesh" to Southern arms, threatening Federal communications and bolstering the forces being gathered by recruiters such as Porter and Poindexter. Indeed, Union soldiers reported that the countryside was "greatly excited" about the order, and "a considerable number left their homes with intention to again in some way resist its execution." The necessity to declare oneself loyal or disloyal no doubt was one reason why the Confederate recruiters were as successful as they were in enlisting men into service behind enemy lines. It may also explain Porter's resiliency in the face of his defeats at Moore's Mill and Kirksville.

The EMM's military record was decidedly mixed. The Seventy-second and Seventy-fourth EMM were called from their homes on January 7, 1863, and fought bravely the next day for several hours against Jo Shelby's regular Confederate troops at the Battle of Springfield. Captain Milton Burch made

good use of the EMM's local knowledge in locating the enemy in his skirmishes in southwest Missouri. Other units failed to stand up against attacks by hard-bitten guerrillas and ran at the first shot. Some examples show their varied experiences.

George Bingham. Bingham, a wagon maker, was captain of Company H, Seventy-first EMM, at Arrow Rock, Saline County, 1862–63. On the recommendation of his cousin, Missouri state treasurer and renowned artist George Caleb Bingham, George Bingham was allowed to raise a company of militia under General Order No. 107. His men fought valiantly at Glasgow in October 1864 but were captured by a superior Confederate force and then paroled. *Wilson's Creek National Battlefield*.

Captain George Bingham, a wagon maker from Arrow Rock, commanded Company H of the Seventy-first EMM. Bingham was a first cousin of George Caleb Bingham, the Missouri artist, politician and state treasurer in the provisional government during the war. Company H served intermittently from August 1862 to May 1863. During that time, Bingham's company saw no combat, as it was engaged primarily in guarding towns. In August 1864, Bingham and a few of his men were recalled into active duty as a "provisional" company under General Order No. 107, which provided for the creation of companies of the best men from the EMM to assist in controlling growing internal unrest that preceded Sterling Price's raid into Missouri.

When Price entered western Missouri, Bingham led his 85 men to Glasgow, where they came under the command of Colonel Chester Harding Jr. On October 14, they were sent to reestablish telegraph communications with St. Louis but were driven back by an enemy force of 250 men. The next day, about 40 men from Bingham's company were detailed as pickets to guard a bridge over the creek on the Boonville road and to warn of the Confederate advance. After repulsing several attacks, they were in danger of being surrounded and escaped to Macon City. Bingham, however, remained in Glasgow with the rest of his men. Outnumbered three to one, the Federals fought off the Confederates for three hours but finally surrendered and were paroled.

The Seventy-first included two companies of seventy German Americans from eastern Lafayette and western Saline Counties. Their fate was much more melancholy. Companies B and C served from August to December 1862. A few men were involved in a skirmish with guerrillas near Wellington (west of Lexington), but most—like Company H—saw no action. While they were away on duty, guerrillas (perhaps led by Dave Poole, a Lafayette County man noted for his hatred of the Germans) attacked a gathering at an infant baptism. They took eleven men captive and killed two of them. The guerrillas shot three more men before leaving the area. In July 1863, Poole and the guerrillas returned. This time, they captured and executed four members of the regiment.

But the worst raid came in 1864. A party of at least one hundred guerrillas—again led by Dave Poole—camped at Brownsville (now Sweet Springs) on October 9. The next day, Germans, warned of the guerrillas' approach, gathered at a Lutheran church near present-day Concordia. Some of them had been in the EMM, but none had seen any action before.

They divided into two groups, neither armed with more than shotguns. One group tried unsuccessfully to ambush Poole and his men. Some blasted away at the horsemen, and other fired into the air because "they couldn't

Glenn House, Paris, Missouri. This hotel, built in 1855, had fourteen-inch solid brick exterior walls and nine-inch solid brick interior walls. It made the perfect fort for Captain W.E. Fowkes and his Seventieth EMM on October 15, 1864. They held off a force six times their size for three hours until the Rebels threatened to burn the building. The hotel survived until 1974, when it was torn down. *Wilson's Creek National Battlefield.*

have a man's life on their conscience," even a man as ruthless as Poole. The guerrillas suffered no losses, and the party scattered into the brush.

A second group of about twenty-five Germans rode toward the present town of Emma, where they encountered Poole's men, now reinforced by additional guerrillas. The Germans managed to kill one guerrilla and wound a few others, but it was an uneven fight. All but one of the Germans was killed, chased down like rabbits. The Rebels not only shot the men but also beat their heads in with gun butts and clubs. With all resistance crushed, the guerrillas went on a destructive spree, burning homes and killing even more men. Once they were finished, the guerrillas rejoined Price.

Company C, Seventieth EMM, from Monroe County, was activated in 1864 under the leadership of Captain W.E. Fowkes. On August 30, 1864, Captain Fowkes, with about sixty men, searched for and found guerrillas in southwest Monroe County. They killed one and wounded another. Their most well-known fight, however, came on October 15, when a force of four hundred guerrillas led by Colonel Wash McDaniel and Major Elliot Majors rode into Paris. Fowkes holed up in the Glenn House Hotel with fifty-five of his men and nine from the Ninth Cavalry MSM. They held off the raiders until 8:00 p.m., but the Rebels set fire to a nearby building and threatened to burn down the hotel. Fowkes's wife was sent into the Glenn House to convince him to surrender to avoid a needless loss of life. The Rebels left the next afternoon. The district EMM commander, General J.B. Douglass, sent ever more urgent messages to headquarters requesting reinforcements and artillery to counter the attacks, finally prompting an exasperated reply: "You have force enough to destroy Majors. You shut yourself up and telegraph about Majors' doing what he pleases in your district. Don't you think if you killed a few of them it would improve the condition of your district?"

Gamble sought to enhance the quality of the EMM by selecting the best men to serve in units called the Provisional Enrolled Missouri Militia (PEMM). The PEMM was better equipped and better led and often fought side by side with the MSM and regular volunteers. Some of the regiments, particularly the Sixth and Seventh PEMM, distinguished themselves. But these soldiers, like those in the EMM, were not exactly volunteers themselves—a point Radical legislators made. By the end of the war, many men from both the PEMM and the EMM had enlisted in regular Missouri volunteer regiments raised to satisfy demands for more troops for Federal service.

THE PAW PAW MILITIA

In the summer of 1863, northwest Missouri was largely denuded of Union troops. The insatiable demands of General Grant for more and more men for the Vicksburg Campaign siphoned off most of the regular volunteer units. The MSM regiments were fighting guerrillas in more active areas of operations in central and southern Missouri. Even the numbers in the EMM were down. Large swaths of northwest Missouri were hotbeds of Secessionist sympathies, and thus those men were ineligible for membership. Most Union men either bought their way out by paying the thirty-dollar commutation fee or had already joined the volunteers or the MSM. Those who were in the EMM were especially poorly led and equipped.

The troubles in northwest Missouri came from jayhawkers, not Confederate guerrillas. Governor Gamble sought an innovative but controversial solution—arm former Confederate soldiers who had returned home and registered as "disloyal." He authorized Colonels James Moss and John Scott to enroll these men into the Eighty-first and Eighty-second EMM, mostly from Platte and Clinton Counties. These regiments became known as the Paw Paw Militia, supposedly taking their name because they camped among the eponymous bushes in the river bottoms or, as others unkindly suggested, because of the sympathy they held for the bushwhackers who also camped there.

From the first, the enrollment of the Paw Paws generated a good deal of political heat. Radicals were appalled that the government would arm former Confederates and rely on them for anything. Indeed, the concern was so great that it filtered up to President Lincoln, who specifically asked about their reliability. Initially at least, the Paw Paws proved effective in stopping depredations from Kansas. Local commanders boasted that the area had never been so quiet during the war. Militia officers, hauled before the Missouri Radicals' Committee to Investigate the Conduct and Management of the Militia, testified that northwest Missouri "was in a very disturbed condition" until the Paw Paws were organized, but now it "was much more peaceable."

There were still misgivings, though, among the Radical politicians and residents of the area. Moss, for example, was suspected of being a secret Secessionist sympathizer. And why not? His second cousin was Jefferson Davis, and his brother-in-law was the renowned John C. Calhoun ("Coon") Thornton, a Confederate hero of the Siege of Lexington, as well as at that very moment a clandestine recruiter for the army. Nothing was ever proved, but Coon Thornton roamed Platte County with impunity. By the summer of 1864, he had brought to the Southern banner an estimated five hundred men, about half of whom were Paw Paws who had once again switched their allegiance.

Matters came to a head on July 10, 1864, when Thornton marched into Platte City. Five companies of Paw Paws surrendered instead of defending the town, and fifteen minutes later, they signed up with their former opponents. Thornton was still basking in this coup three days later when exasperated Federals caught up with him. He had just delivered a stirring address in Camden Point at a picnic celebrating the new recruits when one thousand Kansas and Colorado cavalry thundered into town. The Rebels scattered, but the Union forces ruthlessly hunted them down. They later claimed to have killed two hundred and wounded one hundred of Thornton's men. The Paw Paw experiment came to an end.

Chapter 8

"Such Inhuman Wretches Deserve No Mercy"

"We Got After the Bushwhackers"

On January 5, 1863, George Wolz wrote to his brother, John, musing about Christmas and reporting that he had seen a "god meney good lokin girls" in Springfield. He told John he wished they could "go sacken [skating] wit you and huge the girls and dance wit the girls." Instead, the company was camped in winter quarters about two miles from Springfield.

In early January 1863, Captain Milton Burch, Fourteenth Cavalry MSM, led a scout into northern Arkansas. He captured two Confederate soldiers, who told him that General John Marmaduke was heading toward Springfield with six thousand men. Burch immediately notified General Egbert Brown.

In response to Burch's information, Brown gathered what troops he could to defend the town. He ordered battalions from the Fourth and Fourteenth Cavalry MSM to come to Springfield immediately. He called up the Seventy-second and Seventy-fourth EMM. Brown also pressed into service about one hundred convalescents from the hospital, dubbed the Quinine Brigade, and placed them under command of Captain Charles McAfee of the Third Cavalry MSM. Altogether, Brown was able to muster about two thousand men to oppose Marmaduke.

After an intensely cold night, Marmaduke advanced on Springfield at about 10:00 a.m. on January 8. The Third Cavalry, with the battalions from the other militia cavalry units, held Brown's left, opposite Jo Shelby's

Iron Brigade. The regiment's skirmishers exchanged desultory fire with the Rebels until they were driven in about 2:00 p.m.

The fight shifted to the Union right, where the Confederates found a ravine providing them sufficient cover to attack the EMM troops stationed on that side of town. For nearly thirteen hours, the battle shifted back and forth around a two-story brick college building and a nearby cemetery. Wolz and the other Union soldiers lay on their weapons all night, waiting for a renewed attack the next day. But Marmaduke decided to break off the engagement. Union casualties were put at 14 killed, 146 wounded and 5 captured. Marmaduke said he lost 19 killed, 105 wounded and 26 captured or missing. Wolz wrote to his brother that he saw 20 Confederate dead left on the battlefield the next day.

The Battle of Springfield was Wolz's last action with the Third Cavalry. As part of a reorganization of the militia units, all of the men of the Third Cavalry whose enlistment had not expired were transferred to the Sixth or Seventh Cavalry MSM. Wolz was assigned to Company L, Seventh Cavalry MSM, commanded by Captain Marlin Henslee, effective February 15, 1863. Wolz joined his new regiment in Greenfield.

In late March, the Seventh moved to Carthage, Missouri. Wolz noted that the region was practically deserted, although "a few Seceshist fameleys stil lives hear." After the excitement of the battle with Marmaduke's men, the regiment took up routine patrolling once again, searching for guerrillas. Wolz went on two scouts with his new company. He reported that they did not have much trouble with bushwhackers, but a few of them did shoot at the Federals from the brush. Despite prior orders that suggested that they take no prisoners, the cavalrymen captured two bushwhackers—"very notorious characters"—during their stay. On April 22, under a flag of truce, the battalion commander, Lieutenant Colonel Thomas Crittenden, agreed to exchange the prisoners for men being held by the guerrillas. It was something not to be seen again.

On May 13, Major Edward Eno left Newtonia with eighty-four men from Companies I, K, L and M of the Seventh Cavalry under Captain Henslee and Captain Squire Ballew, as well as one hundred men from his own regiment, on a scout along Centre Creek. He was searching for guerrilla Tom Livingston, who before the war worked lead mines there in Newton and Jasper Counties. Eno ordered Captain Ballew, with fifty men, to make a wide swing west past Neosho to Sherwood (near present-day Joplin) "driving the brush thoroughly." Then Ballew was supposed take up a position at French Point, west of Carthage and near one of Livingston's mines. Eno

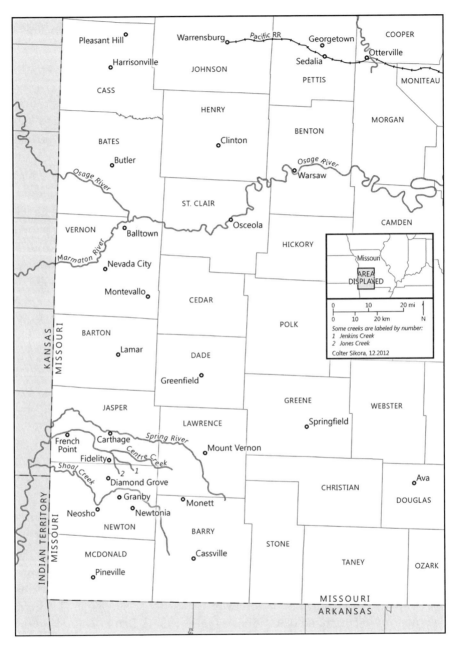

Southwest Missouri during the Civil War. Southwest Missouri was a gateway for raiders from Arkansas. The lead mines at Granby and along Centre Creek were guerrilla Tom Livingston's home and the area of his principal operations. George Wolz and the Seventh Cavalry MSM "got after the bushwhackers" in this area in 1863. *Map by Colter Sikora.*

would come down Centre Creek from the east until he met Ballew, hopefully driving any guerrillas they met into the latter's hands.

On the morning of May 16, Major Eno again divided his command. In an extended skirmish line, Henslee's men (including Wolz) rode down the prairie on the north side of the creek; Captain Jacob Caissart, with forty men of the Eighth Cavalry, took the south side. Eno led the remainder along Centre Creek itself. The flanking lines got far ahead of Eno because he had to traverse the bluffs and rough ground in the timber in the valley.

Early in the afternoon, Henslee came upon Livingston's pickets four miles south of Carthage. The pickets fired and then fled west. Wolz wrote home that "we got after the bushwhackers and drove them down Senter Creek about five miles." Henslee's company crossed Centre Creek and joined the southern column. Livingston's men took cover in a log house and in dense brush one and a half miles east of French Point. For fifteen minutes, the militia and Rebels fought at close range. In the smoke and the noise, it was difficult to tell friend from foe in the underbrush because many of the guerrillas were wearing captured Federal uniforms.

Henslee's horse bolted, and he shot through the startled guerrillas. He finally got turned around and galloped back, firing his pistol and killing one of the Rebels as he went through their lines from the rear. The guerrillas captured four Federal soldiers. Then, Wolz wrote to his brother, the bushwhackers "poured the shout from the house[.] we fit them awhile and the[y] croud on us so close that we had to retrut[.] we cept up the fire as we retreated[.] we retreated to the prarie and then formed[.] I found out that my mare was giten lame I got a mull that the rider had got woud and had fel of and by this by this tyme Major Eno came up and we went after them. they had left the bate feald[.] we found five dead."

Major Eno led the militiamen in hot pursuit and recaptured most of the soldiers taken by the guerrillas. Expecting at any moment to hear Ballew's guns at French Point, Eno instead found the "bank was still wet with the water carried out by Livingston's crossing." Ballew was nowhere to be found. Either he disobeyed orders (Eno's view) or he misunderstood them (his story). In any event, Livingston got away. Ballew took the blame. However, he remained in command of Company I until 1864, when he was dismissed for incompetence. One of the three officers on the board that considered his case was Major Edward Eno.

The next day, Eno searched along the Spring River for Livingston. He followed the Rebels' trail for a few miles, but it became apparent that the quarry split up into small groups. The cavalry "kept moving slowly through the brush and over by-roads, crossing and re-crossing the creek…almost continually fighting them, starting up scattered squads of 4 to 10, chasing and firing on them." Wolz's company followed some of Livingston's men "down to the ingoton [Indian] nation," then returned to the battlefield.

The combined Seventh and Eighth Cavalry lost four men killed: Henry Maxey from Wolz's Company L, Sergeant Charles Credé from Company M (who reportedly was captured, stripped naked and shot), Winston Darnaby from Company M and Horace Palmer from the Eighth Cavalry. Wolz's fellow Grundy County man, John Anderson, was wounded in the leg. Another man was wounded in the foot. Wolz could not get his mare into camp, and he "left her thirty mylls from cap at a house." The horse was finally reported killed. Wolz wrote to his brother that the Rebels had seven dead "that I know of," how many were wounded "I don't know."

Wolz's company returned to routine scouts, first from Newtonia and then from McElhany (south of Neosho). The only combat he reported in his next letter home was the killing of some bushwhackers by "rangers," as some companies of the Fourteenth (later Eighth) Cavalry MSM called themselves.

On June 19, Wolz was back in Newtonia. The Seventh continued to scout through southwest Missouri because, as Wolz wrote, there "is a good many bushwhackers in this part of the country." Federals killed five of them and (perhaps) to their surprise found a letter in one of the dead Rebel's pockets from a woman whom the Seventh had been protecting. Farmers were fleeing north and south to escape the violence. Wolz noted that the guerrillas would burn one house, and the Federals would retaliate by burning two. Nevertheless, Wolz—ever the farmer's son—recorded that the wheat and the cherries were ripe. On June 21, Wolz wrote that the Federals killed nine more Rebels on a scout to Cassville, and a lieutenant of the rangers killed three more when they surprised a group in camp.

Tom Livingston met his end before the summer was over. On July 11, a detachment of thirteen men from the Twenty-sixth EMM was in Stockton's brick courthouse listening to a political speech. Suddenly, a group of horsemen rode up to the building at top speed. Livingston, armed with a revolver attached to a rifle stock, reined in his horse and fired just as the militia slammed the heavy doors closed. One of the EMM shot him. The gun battle continued for several minutes. At last, the militia broke out. Livingston lay wounded outside the door. As he tried to rise, a soldier grabbed Livingston's weapon and broke the rifle's stock over his head. Other militiamen riddled his body with musket and pistol balls. The guerrillas scattered with their wounded.

After one last sweep led by the Seventh's Colonel John Philips turned up nothing, the regiment was ordered to Sedalia. It arrived there on August 10, and shortly afterward, Company L was ordered to Versailles. It was a quiet sector. The men went on daily scouts, but Wolz reported to his brother that "ther isent much trouble here[.] ther is some stealing of horses and the[y] stole some money from a man last nite." Mostly, he said, they ate watermelon, apples, plums and peaches and dressed up to "chat the girls."

"YOU'RE A DEAD DOG IF YOU FAIL TO ISSUE THE ORDER"

As part of the reorganization and consolidation of the MSM in early 1863, Bazel Lazear's Twelfth Cavalry MSM was broken up and reassigned. Three companies went to the new Third Cavalry MSM, and five went to the new Fifth Cavalry MSM. Lazear, however, did not follow them to either regiment. He was reassigned to the First Cavalry MSM in central Missouri.

After a long ride from Jackson, Missouri (where his wife came to visit him for Christmas), Lazear arrived at his new post in Harrisonville, severely sunburned but eager to go. As with Colonel Jackson, Lazear found his new commander, Colonel James McFerran, a "very poor military man." Cass County was beautiful, but Lazear noted that "nearly everybody has left it… [except] some scattering thieves and Bushwhackers here killing and stealing wherever they can." He had as much trouble from local Radical Union men as from guerrillas. The conflict arose when Lazear's men intercepted forty-two runaway slaves from Johnson County on their way to Kansas. He held them for twenty-four hours without food or shelter from the rain. After taking all of their meager possessions, Lazear sent four back to their master and told the rest to get out of his lines.

The next month, Lazear was in Warrensburg, "a very fine town before the war but it is the dirtiest filthiest place I ever saw." Like Cass County, Johnson County was desolate: one-third of the houses were destroyed, and few civilians lived there. Shortly after his arrival, Lazear arrested and, with a good deal of uneasiness, jailed twenty local "rebel ladies" as part of a district-wide dragnet to deny assistance to the guerrillas. The new commander, General Thomas Ewing Jr., explained his reasons to General Schofield: "About two-thirds of the families on the occupied farms [of the border tier of Missouri

A company of the Twenty-fifth Missouri Infantry, later consolidated into the First Missouri Engineers. In 1863, Frank James killed four men from the Twenty-fifth near Missouri City. Soldiers followed him to the family farm, where they beat his younger brother, Jesse, and hanged his stepfather until he revealed Frank's hiding place. The James family got partial revenge by murdering twenty-three unarmed soldiers at Centralia, including seven from this regiment. *Wilson's Creek National Battlefield.*

counties] are kin to the guerrillas, and are actively and heartily engaged in feeding, clothing, and sustaining them. The presence of these families is the cause of the presence there of the guerrillas."

Lazear moved yet again, this time to Lexington. While there, he tried out new tactics against the guerrillas. He sent out men at night on foot to cover the roads. When a party of guerrillas came along, the Federals gunned them down at close range. "Wonder how they like bushwhacking?" he mused.

The First Cavalry's routine patrolling was rudely interrupted by Quantrill's deadly raid on Lawrence, Kansas, on August 21, 1863. William Quantrill gathered a band of nearly four hundred guerrillas at the Perdee farm on the Blackwater River in Johnson County. His aim was to take revenge on the Jayhawkers by destroying the center of their activities, Lawrence. Although the town had been on alert earlier, a scout now found it vulnerable to an attack. A terrible incident sealed the guerrillas' resolve. Federal soldiers detained several women on charges of providing food and clothing to guerrillas. Many of the women were related to guerrillas in Quantrill's band, including Bill Anderson and John McCorkle. They were held in a makeshift jail in the Kansas City home of artist and state treasurer George Caleb Bingham. On August 13, the building collapsed, killing one of Anderson's sisters and four other women and leaving the survivors "dreadfully mangled and crushed."

The cause of the collapse was never satisfactorily explained, but the guerrillas were convinced that the Union soldiers deliberately murdered their womenfolk. Writing years later, McCorkle said, "We could stand no more…my God, did we not have enough to make us desperate and thirst for revenge?… [O]ur innocent and beautiful girls had been murdered in a most foul, brutal, savage and damnable manner. We were determined to have revenge."

At dawn, the guerrillas burst into Lawrence, firing their revolvers and yelling. They gunned down more than twenty unarmed African American recruits camped there. Groups of guerrillas systematically went from house to house, calling the men and boys to come out and then killing them. They took money, jewelry and any other goods they could carry away and then burned the homes. At last, the guerrillas returned to the business district, where they set the remaining buildings on fire. After four hours of killing and plunder, Quantrill decided it was time to leave. He left the town in flames and nearly two hundred dead bodies behind.

Kansans were furious. Senator Jim Lane, who escaped death by hiding in a cornfield in his nightshirt, telegraphed Lincoln that he was organizing a Kansas militia to attack Missouri even if he had to fight his way through Union troops to do it. At a tempestuous meeting with General Ewing, where the latter said he would issue a directive deporting Southern sympathizers, Lane snapped, "You're a dead dog if you fail to issue the order as agreed between us."

On August 25, 1863, Ewing issued one of the most famous and controversial orders of the war, General Order No. 11. The directive required all persons leave Jackson, Cass, Bates and the northern half of Vernon Counties within fifteen days, unless they could prove they were loyal. Loyal citizens could remain, but they had to move to within one mile of four military posts. As if that was not drastic enough, Ewing ordered Kansas cavalry into the affected areas to enforce the evacuation.

The residents were caught totally unprepared. They had little or no transport and little idea of where they could go anyway. Between ten thousand and twenty thousand civilians, mostly families of Confederate soldiers or guerrillas, jammed the roads to the east and south. Most, if not all, of the Union families in the affected area had already left their homes. By the end of September 1863, the entire countryside south of Kansas City was marked by the remains of chimneys from the burned-out homes.

While the civilians were trying to leave western Missouri, Union commanders gathered troops from all over western and central Missouri to root out the culprits. The Kansas cavalry, including the notorious "Red Legs" (so named for their red leather gaiters), led by George Hoyt (one of John Brown's defense counsel), executed the raiders they caught on the spot. Lazear led two hundred men into northeast Cass County, where they caught up with Quantrill's main body. The guerrillas, in captured blue coats, tried to pass themselves off as Union troops, but Lazear saw through that trick. He killed five of Quantrill's men there and five later as they fled the area.

The hunt continued for a week, when the exhausted Federals returned to their camps to refit. Ewing reported that they had killed eighty of the raiders. The retribution continued. Lazear wrote to his wife on September 10 that "yesterday I had one publically shot. He was a prisoner we took the other evening after we had the fight with Quantrill and was in the Lawrence raid. He is the second prisoner I have had shot and I will have every one of them shot I can get hold of, as such inhuman wretches deserve no mercy and should be shot down like dogs where ever found."

Lazear's sympathy for the families affected by Order No. 11 was measured:

> [T]here is hundreds of people leaving their homes from this country and god knows what is to become of them. It is heart sickening to see what I have seen since I have been back here. A desolated country and women & children, some of them allmost naked. Some on foot and some in old wagons. Oh god. What a sight to see in this once peaceable and happy country…
>
> [Coming down from Kansas City on the boat I] saw the secesh women and children and the few men fleeing from the wrath to come…The boat was crowded full of them and god knows where they are all going for I dont nor do I care so we can get rid of them in Missouri for I think if we get rid of the women and Bushwhackers that it will not be hard to get rid of them. A great many think that was a very unjust and cruel order of General Ewings but I think it was one of the best orders that has been issued and I think that it will have a good effect…And if we cant get the Bushwhackers out of here soon this region will be much the same way. I intend to send all the families of Bushwhackers out of this and Johnson county just as fast as I can give them notice to leave.

Charles McAfee. McAfee was captain of Company E, Third Cavalry MSM. In January 1863, he was placed in a command of one hundred convalescents from the hospital, a makeshift company known as the "Quinine Brigade" that played a key role in the Battle of Springfield. Transferred to the Sixth Cavalry MSM, McAfee's luck ran out in October 1863 when his command was surrounded and captured at Neosho by General Jo Shelby. *Wilson's Creek National Battlefield.*

Just as Quantrill was leaving Missouri to winter in Texas, another threat materialized on the southern border. General Jo Shelby led one thousand men on a six-week raid that again threw the western portion of the state into turmoil. On October 4, Captain Charles McAfee of the Quinine Brigade fame, and now in the Sixth Cavalry MSM, entered Neosho at about 8:00 a.m. Just south of town, he ran into three hundred Confederates. McAfee retreated to the town, and when the Rebels entered from the other side, his men took cover in the brick courthouse. They held out until Shelby's artillery lobbed four shells into the building. After some dickering, McAfee surrendered, losing all of his baggage and arms.

Shelby pressed on, skirmishing with Federal troops all the way to Boonville. There he encountered Bazel Lazear's First Cavalry. Shelby withdrew to Dug Ford on the Lamine River, where the two forces clashed on the "rugged and precipitous" banks of that river. Shelby once again withdrew, this time to Marshall. Lazear followed him and, on October 13, engaged in a three-hour firefight. The Confederates charged Lazear's dismounted troopers several times without success.

In the meantime, Wolz and Company L, which had joined the pursuit, came up as part of four thousand men under the district commander,

General Egbert Brown. One battalion of the Seventh under Major Thomas Houts attacked the enemy across a bridge east of Marshall. Colonel Philips led the rest of his men, including Company L, "through dense underbrush, over ravines and rugged hills" to Shelby's left flank northwest of town. He dismounted his men and sent Company L to support a section of the First Artillery MSM. The remaining men advanced on Shelby's position. Shelby decided to make his escape to the northwest toward his hometown of Waverly.

Philips mounted the nine companies he had (the others were with Major Houts) and pursued the Rebels across the prairie. At one point, both sides drew up in line of battle, and Philips charged. Once again, Shelby slipped away, Philips reported, "going at full run, and while we shouted and shot at him, he used his hats on his jaded horses, throwing overboard every weight (not the arms) that beset him and retarded his movements." Shelby, not surprisingly, reported it differently, writing that his men mounted in "splendid order" and escaped the Federals who "gave away in terror."

However it was reported, it was a crushing defeat for Shelby. He managed to get back to Arkansas only because of a desultory pursuit. Lazear wrote to his wife in disgust that Shelby's men "ought to have been all captured" if only his superiors had followed his advice, "but I suppose Brig. Generals did not like to act on the suggestion of a Lt. Col. and therefore all the good that might have come out of the information I gave them and the suggestions was lost to the country." Federal losses were relatively light given the intensity of the fight. Lazear, however, mourned the death of his beloved horse, Button, shot twice and mortally wounded at Marshall.

"My First Shot Gave Them Hell"

Two Medals of Honor were awarded in the guerrilla war. Both were earned by brothers in the Third Wisconsin Cavalry: James and George Pond.

James was an ardent abolitionist. Before he turned twenty, he was fighting beside John Brown in Kansas. He was a Wide Awake and edited an antislavery newspaper. On October 6, 1863, James, two companies of the Third Wisconsin Cavalry and a company of the Second Kansas Colored Infantry were eating lunch outside the walls of "Fort" Blair, near Baxter

Springs, Kansas, when Quantrill's men surprised them. Pond and his men ran back to the fort, really no more than a half-finished log fence surrounding some tents. There was a small howitzer just outside the entrenchment. Pond called for men to help him shoot it, but none was willing to expose himself as the Rebels' gunfire was pelting the logs: "This made me a little mad, and I jumped over myself, and let them shoot at me until I broke open a box of shell with an axe and loaded and fired…three times by myself, without swabbing or thumbing, and having no rammer, I was obliged to use an axe-helve. My first shot give them hell, and made them fall back over the hill, killing one horse and man."

After a thirty-minute firefight, there was silence. Pond could not imagine why. The guerrillas had found a better target: district commander General James Blunt's headquarters entourage. As Blunt approached what he thought was an honor guard, the guerrillas, many of them wearing blue Union uniforms, formed a line of battle. The Rebels opened fire. Some soldiers charged Quantrill. Suddenly, two hundred more guerrillas charged into the mêlée. The general barely escaped, but most of his escort did not. The guerrillas killed eighty-five cavalrymen, "nearly all shot through the head, most of them shot from five to seven times each, horribly mangled, charred and blackened by fire," including his headquarters band. It was the regiment's worst defeat, but for the heroic stand that saved his men, Pond was awarded the Medal of Honor in 1898.

George Pond disliked garrison duty and much preferred scouting or courier duty. May 16, 1864, found him in Vernon County. Word came that Henry Taylor's guerrillas were raiding homes in the area. Believing it to be only a small group, George and two others rode to investigate. Upon reaching the Lewis Ury place, they discovered that guerrillas had taken Ury and his son, Joe—a Union scout whom they especially disliked—as prisoners. Just as the Rebels were leaving, George led the Federals in a rush, pouring a hail of fire into the guerrillas with his revolver. When the shooting began, Joe grabbed a heavy piece of wood and clubbed one of his captors. The rest fled, but before they left, the bushwhackers mortally wounded Lewis in the thigh. George Pond received his Medal of Honor in 1899.

Homer Pond, a third brother serving in the Third Wisconsin, received no medals, but he got something more important out of the affair at the Ury farm. He married Lewis Ury's daughter, Barbara, in January 1865.

"I Am Pleased to State Every Last Man of Us Was Arrested"

Given that Governor Gamble, a conservative Unionist, appointed its officers, the command structure of the MSM was largely conservative itself. During the first year of its existence, that posed few problems. But as Radicals began their ascent to power in Missouri, many of the MSM senior officers found themselves under political fire for their harsh treatment of the more radical civilians, their alleged soft treatment of Secessionist civilians and their protective stance toward slavery, which was still legal in the state.

The Seventh Cavalry was certainly not immune to these pressures. Its first serious run-in with higher authorities, however, came from revenge taken by some of its members against suspected Secessionists. A patrol from Company H led by Lieutenant Gustavus Westhoff shot and killed two men in early August. Other patrols from Company G killed six more citizens and just two bushwhackers in the first ten days of August. An investigation commissioned by General Brown disclosed the cause of these depredations, if not a justification. Some of the Seventh's soldiers had been part of or had family members who had been part of a Home Guard unit massacred at Cole Camp on June 20, 1861. Local Rebels surrounded them and killed thirty-six men, leaving sixty-two children fatherless that day. The Secessionists either remained in the area or, after serving in the Confederate army or with guerrillas, returned by 1863. The provost marshal suggested that some of the problem was caused by excessive drinking. That may be true. Lieutenant Westhoff died on August 31, 1863, of delirium tremens at the age of thirty-seven.

Lieutenant Colonel Crittenden came under severe criticism from the Radicals in the Missouri legislature for his handling of a trial involving two citizens. Soldiers from the Seventh Cavalry who, as George Wolz noted, spent a lot of time in 1863 searching for horse thieves, arrested a Dr. Zimmerman and a Mr. Hamilton for stealing horses belonging to a known Southern sympathizer. They were convicted by a drumhead court-martial—a summary affair with no official legal sanction in army regulations, sometimes used by both Union and Confederate officers to provide the semblance of legality. A firing squad from Company M executed them a few days later.

Radicals criticized Crittenden for the informality of the proceedings. They noted that the civil courts in the county where the theft occurred were in "full" operation (although there had been no trials held there in three

Thomas Crittenden. A lieutenant colonel of the Seventh Cavalry MSM during the war, Crittenden was elected governor of Missouri in 1880. He fought at the Big Blue against Confederate general John Marmaduke, who was elected to succeed him in 1884. Crittenden offered a reward for Jesse James, resulting in his murder by Bob Ford in 1882. Frank James surrendered to Crittenden personally in the governor's office in Jefferson City shortly afterward. *Library of Congress.*

years) and that there was therefore no reason to resort to military justice of any kind. Moreover, the men stole only from Secessionists anyway and for that reason probably would have been acquitted in a civil court. The legislators' outrage was probably fueled by the fact that Dr. Zimmerman was a supporter of Charles Drake, the leading Radical in the state.

In another case, Radicals went after General Brown for the prosecution and conviction of John Maddox, a farmer from Johnson County and the captain of an irregular group of Unionists that called itself "Company Q" or the "Clear Fork Rangers." Maddox claimed that he raised the company when the MSM refused to provide any protection to Unionists. The soldiers alleged that Company Q used that as an excuse to terrorize its enemies—many of them known or suspected to be Southern sympathizers—and to steal their money, weapons and other property. Maddox was arrested and tried before a military commission in Jefferson City.

Radicals criticized the proceedings because most of the witnesses against Maddox were suspected Secessionists or related to Rebel soldiers or guerrillas. Given that they were the accused's victims, this reproach seems illogical. Moreover, the critics were scandalized when the military commission paid three dollars a day to put up the wives of Rebels who were witnesses for the prosecution in a Jefferson City hotel during the trial. One Radical claimed that the principal witness against Maddox was "habitual malicious liar," a conclusion he reinforced by a personal "minute phrenological examination" of the man's head. Perhaps under political pressure—one of Maddox's strongest supporters was the Radical state representative from his county—Union headquarters set aside the verdict.

These conflicts were but a symptom of a growing ideological divide in the state, not over the treatment of civilians but rather over slavery. The political convulsions that surrounded the emancipation of Missouri slaves split the Unionists into several different groups: Snowflakes (reactionaries who opposed emancipation in any form), Claybanks (conservatives such as Hamilton Gamble who came to support gradual emancipation) and Charcoals (Radicals such as Charles Drake who demanded immediate emancipation). The acrimony was so fierce that an exasperated Lincoln wrote that there were Missourians "who are for the Union with, not without, slavery; those who are for it without, not with; those for it with or without, but prefer it with; and those for it with or without, but prefer it without. Among these, again, is a subdivision of those who are for gradual, but not for immediate, and those who are for immediate, but not gradual, extinction of slavery."

Slavery was the flashpoint that plunged Missouri into the border war in the 1850s and into the Civil War along with other states. As a border state where slavery was an important aspect of its economy, Missouri was in an unusual position. Because it had not seceded, Lincoln's Emancipation Proclamation of January 1, 1863, did not apply to Missouri slaves. Regardless of their formal legal status, the number of slaves in Missouri declined by 35 percent in the first two years of the war. Most of them gained their freedom by escaping to the free states of Kansas, Iowa or Illinois.

What to do with the black refugees who flooded the Federal camps during the war was a problem that plagued Union commanders from the beginning. They vacillated between treating them as "contraband"—property that, if used to assist the rebellion, could be confiscated—and returning runaways to bondage. The military was supposed to be neutral in such disputes, but its attempts to straddle a fine line between slave owners and antislavery groups were not always successful. Bazel Lazear, as noted earlier, had no sympathy for runaway slaves. He followed Missouri law in returning them to their masters, but many other officers not only refused to send them back but also encouraged them to leave for free states.

Regardless of the attitudes of Missouri militia officers, the officers and men from free states on duty in Missouri were aghast at the peculiar institution and blamed it for what they saw as the state's backward ways. They certainly would do nothing to protect slave owners. In one spectacular instance, some enlisted men helped a family of slaves escape at risk to their own freedom.

The Ninth Minnesota Infantry Regiment arrived at Benton Barracks in October 1863, in the midst of Shelby's raid. Whatever plans that might have been made for its use elsewhere were scrapped, and the regiment boarded a Pacific Railroad train bound for Jefferson City. The Northerners were not impressed by what they saw. The farms, one wrote, "testified only to the inherent shiftlessness of those who occupied and pretended to cultivate them." They found Jefferson City to be a muddy town surrounded by hills and creeks. Their only consolation was that they were told that "there are places where mud is more plenty and everything else more disagreeable."

Shelby burned the Pacific Railroad bridge over the Lamine River near Otterville. The Union command decided that it needed better protection than the EMM could provide. Accordingly, 150 men from Companies C and K were sent there under command of Captain David Wellman. With winter coming on, the men built stout log huts and settled into a daily routine of fatigues and drills.

Francis Merchant. Merchant was the ringleader of the "liberators," thirty-eight enlisted men from the Ninth Minnesota Infantry who forcibly removed a slave family from a Pacific Railroad train at Otterville in November 1863. When Federal officers on the train demanded to know where their officers were, Merchant replied, "We are all officers." Later, when the perpetrators were asked to identify themselves, one veteran proudly recalled that "every last man of us was arrested." *Minnesota Historical Society.*

Early on the morning of November 11, a young black man appeared at camp. He was taken to Company C's headquarters, where he was questioned by its commander, Captain Edwin Ford. The man, named John (his last name was never learned), said that he was a slave owned by Charles Walker. Walker had a farm near Georgetown. Walker had obtained passes to send John and his wife and five children; John's brother, Billey, and his wife; and John's two sisters to Kentucky. There, they were certain to be sold and the family broken up.

Captain Ford listened sympathetically, but there was nothing he could do officially because the military had been ordered not to interfere with loyal slave owners. He told the men gathered around that he and his officers were therefore "going to take a walk," and "the boys could do as they please." Sergeant Francis Merchant went around the camp seeking volunteers to help rescue slaves from being sold by their master. Twenty men from Company C and eighteen from Company K shouldered their rifles and marched to the Otterville railroad station.

At 9:00 a.m., the eastbound train pulled in from Sedalia. The Minnesota soldiers opened the boxcars and found the nine slave women and children John told them would be there. They learned that Walker had shot Billey in the head the night before when he tried to escape.

The conductor demanded to know what the men were doing and asked where their officers were. "We are all officers," one (probably Merchant) replied. Captain Oscar Queen, commander of Company M, Seventh Cavalry MSM, and temporary subdistrict commander, was one of the passengers. Queen confronted Merchant and identified himself. The soldiers told Queen that "they didn't care a damn" who he was and refused to leave the women and children on the train. When the conductor tried to signal the engineer to proceed, a squad of soldiers pointed their muskets at him and cocked them.

The men hid John, the women and the children in the woods south of the tracks. A few of them went to the camp and returned with food and a promise of more later. An indignant Captain Queen stopped the train at the Lamine bridge and insisted on seeing Captain Wellman. Wellman knew nothing of what had happened; Captain Ford was still on his walk. Wellman asked the men where the slaves had gone, but they professed to have last seen them in Otterville. When Queen reached his headquarters, he fired off a telegram to General Brown in Jefferson City. The next morning at formation, Wellman asked anyone who was involved in the incident to step forward three paces. All thirty-eight men did. "I am pleased to state," one wrote fifty years later, "every last man of us was arrested."

The "liberators," as they became known, languished in confinement in Jefferson City for weeks. General Brown was unsure what to do with them. Unbeknownst to anyone at Otterville, General Schofield had issued an order on November 10 prohibiting the transport of slaves outside the state. Radicals in the legislature signed a petition to Brown asking that the liberators be released, offering the reasons (among others) that Walker was actually a Southern sympathizer (he was not) and that the men did not recognize Queen as an officer (unlikely). On January 8, 1864, Brown ordered the prisoners back to their regiment, claiming (falsely) that the slave John had lied to them by telling them that Walker was in the Rebel army. It saved face all around and would have been the end of the matter had not the protests percolated to the floor of the Senate in Washington. There, Minnesota senator Morton Wilkinson called for an inquiry into the "act of military official baseness…by the pro-slavery tyrants who have caused this incarceration." Newly elected Radical Missouri senator B. Gratz Brown agreed, criticizing the military affairs of the state as "disastrously managed." Secretary of War Edward Stanton duly investigated and reported that the soldiers had been returned to duty six weeks before the senatorial fireworks.

The Ninth Minnesota was transferred from Missouri to Memphis. It fought bravely in battles in Mississippi and Alabama. Nine of the liberators died in the war: one killed in action, one mortally wounded, one from disease and six at the Andersonville prison camp. Sergeant Merchant returned to Minnesota, where he became successively a deputy sheriff, chief of police and streetcar driver. He died at age eighty-five in San Francisco. Captain Ford, after returning from his walk, was a successful combat leader. After the war, he moved to Wisconsin, where he worked for the railroad. He lived to the age of ninety-three. No one knows what happened to John or his family. When the men were arrested the next day, there was no one left to help them. Like so many others, these slaves were lost to history.

Chapter 9

"Contesting Every Inch of Ground"

GEORGE WOLZ RIDES A BOAT AND COLLECTS TAXES

The winter and early spring were quiet in Sedalia and Pettis County, where George Wolz and the Seventh Cavalry MSM were stationed. But when the weather warmed up, the grass grew (for forage) and the leaves came out (for cover), the guerrillas returned. The Federals received reports that as many as two hundred were filtering back into their old haunts. The guerrillas resumed their raids on towns, wagon trains, railroad trains, mail carriers and steamboats, and then they disappeared into the dense thickets of western Missouri.

Many of the guerrillas wore Federal uniforms captured from the living or taken from the dead. It made identification so difficult that General Brown issued an order specifying passwords and hand signals so that Union commands would not be fooled by bushwhackers pretending to be friendly cavalry. All units, not just the EMM, were directed to wear a red strip of cloth on their hats on odd-numbered days and a white strip on even days.

The attacks intensified in June. A patrol of fourteen men from Company M, First Missouri Cavalry MSM, led by Corporal Joseph Parman, was ambushed near Kingsville on June 12. It was searching for guerrillas when sixty men in "full Federal uniform…[with] the regular badges worn by our men on their hats and caps" suddenly appeared about fifty yards behind. Parman formed his men into a battle line, but the first volley from the guerrillas dropped five troopers in their tracks. The rest broke and ran for their lives. Parman and one other escaped. The rest were caught a short distance away. Four tried to surrender, but the guerrillas shot them in their eyes. All were stripped, and Corporal Edward Ireland was scalped. Bazel Lazear, on court-martial duty at Jefferson City, lamented to his wife, "It makes me almost sick to hear of our poor boys being killed in that way and I cant hear of no guerrillas being killed." The guerrillas were likely Bill Anderson and his men, formerly part of Quantrill's band but now acting independently. It was just the beginning of an even nastier guerrilla war.

Wolz's Company L, as well as all of the Federal forces in western Missouri, was constantly in the field looking for guerrillas, who appeared to be seeking to get across the Missouri River. On July 8, Major Thomas Houts led a party of 150 men, including 50 from Company L under Captain Henslee in a scout from Warrensburg. On a peaceful Sunday morning, they trailed guerrillas to Wellington. A female slave—"a reliable contraband"—told them that the Rebels had gone to Warder's Church, about two miles southeast of town on Little Sni-A-Bar Creek. She said that "a Hardshell was in the habit of preaching to the 'Brushers'" there.

Captain Henslee took fifty men to investigate. They found the church on a high bluff, reachable only by a bridge across the river and a narrow road to the top. He ordered Sergeant Granville Brassfield with six men to rush the building and get to the other side to cut off any attempt to retreat. Seven or eight guerrillas sat on their horses outside, and a few men were posted as pickets at the bridge. The rest were inside listening to the pastor's "fervent supplication" when the cry of "Fed! Feds!" was raised. The guerrillas drew their revolvers and fired at the charging cavalrymen. Just then the women and children ran outside screaming. Captain Henslee roared at them, "Squat!" They did and the fight continued. John Anderson, who had been wounded in the firefight with Livingston near Carthage the year before, was in Brassfield's party. Riding through a hail of revolver fire, Anderson suffered only three holes in his clothes, and one ball struck his pistol. Fortunately, he had three more revolvers and emptied sixteen shots into the guerrillas. A friend of Wolz's, Corporal Jacob Cozard, was shot in the heel. Five bushwhackers were killed and a sixth mortally wounded.

Orders continued to fly from headquarters as the Federals tried to stem the guerrilla attacks. On July 15, General Brown ordered Major Henry Suess to Kansas City with sixty men, ten of them mounted, and one artillery piece to commandeer the first boat down the river to cooperate with Colonel John

Ford, commander of the Second Colorado Cavalry, who was chasing a party of guerrillas downriver toward Sibley. George Wolz was among those on the steamboat *Fanny Ogden*. For the next fifteen days, the water-bound cavalrymen steamed up and down the Missouri River from Fort Leavenworth to Arrow Rock, destroying boats and skiffs and shooting at guerrillas on the shore. Suess's men finally disembarked at Lexington on July 30. That evening, Wolz visited his friend Cozard at the hospital. Evidently, the wound was not serious, for Cozard was back with Company L by August.

On August 8, Captain Albert Brackman, Company E, Ninth Cavalry MSM, wrote an urgent appeal to General William Rosecrans, the department commander:

> *I just received the news that New Frankfort, Saline County, Mo., has been partly burned down by bushwhackers, and that the inhabitants, consisting mostly of discharged soldiers and soldiers' wives and children, have been ordered to leave the town in less than ten days. The town is a German settlement, and has furnished a whole company for the Ninth Cavalry Missouri State Militia, whom I have the honor to command. I do not know what other outrages have been perpetrated besides the burning, but it is more than probable that the devils have committed some of their wanton atrocities. My men request you to send a body of soldiers to protect their families until they are given an opportunity to take them away. If you think it proper, please let me know what you are going to do for these poor soldiers and their suffering families.*

Suess and his men boarded the *Fanny Ogden* again. He left a detachment (including Wolz) at New Frankfort to make an assessment against Southern sympathizers in Saline County as compensation and resumed cruising the river. Wolz spent the next few days "collecting the taxes" of $16,800 for the damages caused by guerrilla depredations. It was not bad duty for the young cavalryman. He boarded with a "Dutch" family, who supplied him with plenty of bacon and lager beer. After staying in New Frankfort for three weeks, Wolz got on a steamboat for Kansas City to get paid. By mid-September, he was back in Warrensburg.

Wolz had hardly returned when a new challenge arose to the Union hold on Missouri. General Sterling Price led twelve thousand Confederates from Arkansas into southeastern Missouri on September 19. Only half of them were armed, but the remainder included Jo Shelby's tough Iron Brigade. As they worked their way north toward St. Louis and then west toward Jefferson City, the guerrillas stepped up their activities, especially north of the Missouri River.

Bill Anderson's guerrillas managed to slip though the Union forces along the Missouri River and spent much of July, August and September terrorizing the inhabitants of central Missouri. On July 11, they hanged nine Union men in Carroll County. On July 15, they killed one man in Huntsville. Anderson entered Rocheport, a little town on the Missouri River between Columbia and Boonville that he called "my capital." On July 17, his men fired thirty shots into the *War Eagle* as it steamed downriver from Lexington to Jefferson City. No one was hurt, but General Brown ordered that all steamboats carry armed guards. On July 22, Anderson burned the depot at Renick and cut several miles of telegraph line. On July 24, he ambushed a force from the Seventeenth Illinois Cavalry and the local EMM, killing two, both of whom were scalped. They next rode into Shelby and Monroe Counties, burning a 150-foot Hannibal & St. Joseph Railroad bridge over the Salt River near Hunnewell.

On July 30, Anderson returned to the Huntsville area. At a farm outside of town, he hanged a seventy-two-year-old man and demanded to know where his money was kept. The guerrillas cut the man down and whipped him, leaving him for dead. A slave ran into town to inform the man's son, Lieutenant Colonel Alexander Denny of the Forty-sixth EMM, who had to be restrained from going to the rescue and into an obvious trap. Denny's father miraculously survived.

Anderson's brutality increased. His men captured a pursuing militiaman, slit his throat and decapitated him. Anderson cut another captive's ears and nose off before he shot him. A St. Joseph newspaper denounced Anderson as the "most heartless, cold-blooded bushwhacking scoundrel that has operated in Missouri since the outbreak of the war." Despite continued exhortations from Union generals, Federal troops could not find him or, if they did, were soundly repulsed.

At the end of August, Captain Joseph Parke, Lieutenant Columbus Dale and forty-two men from Company E, Fourth Cavalry MSM, crossed the Missouri River at Rocheport looking for guerrillas. They were surprised, and seven of his men were killed. They were found later scalped and their throats cut. Lieutenant Dale was erroneously reported dead.

Anderson lingered in Rocheport in early September. On September 12, a patrol from the Ninth Cavalry MSM stationed at Fayette found five of Anderson's men sitting in a barn, cleaning their revolvers. All were killed. On September 23, Anderson retaliated by scattering an eighty-five-man escort

Lieutenant Columbus Dale, Company E, Fourth Missouri Cavalry MSM. Dale was one of more than one thousand Iowans who signed up in Missouri units. His brother, Douglas, a major in the same regiment, was severely wounded in the wrist in 1862. On October 23, 1864, Lieutenant Dale was shot in the right side while leading a charge up the rocky slopes of the Big Blue River. He died the next day. *Wilson's Creek National Battlefield.*

from the Third Cavalry MSM at Goslin Lane, on the Columbia-Fayette road near Rocheport. Twelve men surrendered but were killed by their captors, along with three black teamsters. A party from the Ninth Cavalry hunted down six of Anderson's men, killed and scalped five and took one, Cave Wyatt, as prisoner. Why he was spared is not recorded.

Anderson decided to teach the Ninth Cavalry a lesson by attacking its camp at Fayette. On the way, he encountered George Todd, who told him that General Sterling Price asked the guerrillas' assistance in disrupting Federal communications in support of his invasion. Anderson, Todd, Quantrill and four hundred guerrillas convened outside Fayette. Anderson and Todd argued for an attack on the town's garrison, but Quantrill cautioned against it. He pointed out that there was a brick courthouse in the town and that the MSM used such buildings as forts. Todd said, "We are going into Fayette no matter what! If you want to come along, all right. If not then you can go back into the woods with the rest of the cowards!" Quantrill left and never went into action in Missouri again.

The attack was a disaster. Although at first unrecognized because they were wearing Federal uniforms, the guerrillas lost the element of surprise when one of their number spotted a black man wearing a blue coat and shot him. The soldiers scrambled into the courthouse, firing into the raiders.

A company of the Ninth Missouri Cavalry MSM in 1864. Note that some of the men are wearing cloth strips on their hats as recognition signals ordered by Federal commanders that summer. On September 24, 150 men of the Ninth Cavalry solidified its reputation as one of the most feared guerrilla hunters by repulsing an assault by 400 guerrillas led by George Todd and Bill Anderson. *State Historical Society of Missouri.*

Unable to take that building, the guerrillas instead determined to take the soldiers' camp on the edge of town. The men of the Ninth were waiting in log cabins. When Anderson and Todd's men got within seventy-five yards, the Federals opened fire. The guerrillas had no chance. They were pinned down and "peppered with bullets," leaving thirteen dead and thirty wounded; the Ninth Cavalry lost two dead. The camp's commander, Captain Sheldon Eaton, crowed over the humiliating defeat inflicted on the Rebels, noting that his boys "knocked and cuffed some of the noted Rebs."

The guerrillas returned to Huntsville the day after the Fayette debacle. Anderson sent a messenger to the Union commander, Lieutenant Colonel Denny, demanding his surrender. Denny, no doubt relishing the opportunity to exact revenge for the torture of his father, replied, "Come and take it." Todd convinced Anderson not to repeat the Fayette disaster. They moved east, burning the North Missouri Railroad station at Allen, and headed toward Paris. But local sympathizers warned them of Federal troops stationed there. After spending the night at Middle Grove, the guerrillas, now numbering about five hundred men, moved south and camped on the farm of M.G. Singleton, a prosperous Southern sympathizer who had been an officer in Price's Missouri State Guard in 1861.

On September 27, Anderson led eighty men into the nearby village of Centralia seeking news of Price and of any Federals who may be trailing them. Even though Centralia was considered a Secessionist stronghold, such distinctions meant little to Anderson. His men ransacked the town. In midmorning, the stage from Columbia pulled in, carrying among its passengers a distinguished gentleman: United States Congressman James Rollins. The guerrillas did not recognize him, and Rollins (who would be captured and released by guerrillas three times during the war) told them that he was a Southern Methodist preacher. The looting of the stagecoach was interrupted by the arrival of the noon train.

Anderson's men stopped the train and ordered the passengers to disembark. Among them were twenty-four unarmed Union soldiers on furlough, most from Sherman's army, which had captured Atlanta one week previously. The guerrillas put the civilians on one side of the tracks and the soldiers on the other. They took their money and valuables, killing two civilians. The soldiers were directed to strip. Anderson called for any sergeants to step forward. Puzzled, Sergeant Thomas Goodman did so. He was taken away, apparently to exchange him for Cave Wyatt, captured by the Federals a few days previously. Anderson nodded, and suddenly the guerrillas opened fire, killing the remainder of the captives. The guerrillas left the bodies in a heap by the railroad tracks and returned to camp, drinking stolen whiskey and celebrating.

That afternoon, Major A.V.E. Johnston and three companies from the Thirty-ninth Missouri Volunteer Infantry rode into town. They had been trailing Anderson and Todd from Paris. Johnston had been a member of the Missouri State Guard but switched sides in December 1861. He joined the Fifty-third EMM in 1862. The local Radical politicians complained that Johnston abused them and helped return slaves to their Secessionist owners, but he was known as an aggressive guerrilla hunter. He was appointed major in the Thirty-ninth Missouri, a unit that was just getting organized in September.

Despite warnings from the townsfolk, Johnston decided to attack the guerrilla camp. As he approached Singleton's farm, some of the Rebels rode about in apparent confusion, luring the Thirty-ninth into a trap. Johnston dismounted his men, left his horse holders at the bottom of a slight rise and went into a line of battle with the remainder just below the crest on the other side. Anderson gave a whoop and waved his hat, and nearly 500 guerrillas poured out of the woods. Johnston's men only fired one volley before the horsemen were on them, firing their revolvers. The guerrillas killed all but 2 or 3 men, who fled back to Centralia. Anderson's men followed them and rooted through the buildings, looking for the cowering survivors. Johnston was killed, along with 122 of his men. Their bodies were found, nearly all shot through the head, and many were scalped and horribly mutilated. Anderson and Todd escaped across the Missouri River, and two weeks later, they met General Price at Boonville. Goodman escaped his captors unharmed and went home to Iowa.

Todd remained with Price as a scout, but Anderson's men went on one last rampage, ostensibly to destroy the North Missouri Railroad bridge over Peruque Creek in St. Charles County. They burned Danville and railroad facilities at High Hill. A few guerrillas got as far as Wentzville, where they mortally wounded Frank Groeblinghoff with a shot in the stomach, mistaking him for a Federal officer, Frederick Grabenhorst, who was then at the Lamine River bridge near Otterville with the Forty-ninth Missouri Infantry.

Captain Louis Benecke, a Shiloh veteran, enlisted his entire EMM company in the Forty-ninth Infantry in 1864. He borrowed $4,000 to arm his men with Spencer carbines because he believed that the Centralia Massacre proved they were outgunned by guerrillas. His spies discovered a guerrilla mail drop in a cottonwood tree, revealing a plan to ambush him and allowing him to turn the tables on his prospective killers. From Louis Benecke, *Historical Sketch of the "Sixties"* (1909).

On October 27, Lieutenant Colonel Samuel Cox, with men from the Fifty-first and Thirty-third EMM, discovered Anderson camped west of Albany in southeast Ray County. They drove in Anderson's pickets east of the village, dismounted and hid in the woods west of town. Cox sent a small force to engage the enemy. They fell back, followed by Anderson and his men, who rode after them at full speed, screaming and shooting. The EMM met them with a volley, downing Anderson with two balls in his head. At first they did not know who they had killed, but a search of his body revealed orders from General Price. Anderson was buried in an unmarked grave near Richmond. As a reward for their actions, the officers and men were allowed to keep the property and money taken from Anderson's corpse.

MAJOR JAMES WILSON: MARTYR OR MURDERER?

On the same day Bill Anderson killed 148 soldiers and civilians at Centralia, General Sterling Price attacked Federal troops led by General Thomas Ewing, of Order No. 11 fame (or infamy), at Fort Davidson near Pilot Knob. Price had been working his way slowly from Arkansas for two weeks. By the time he reached Pilot Knob, Ewing had managed to gather a force in a fort protected by a deep ditch. Price's men made repeated, futile and bloody charges. That night, Ewing slipped away and escaped to Leasburg on the Southwest Branch of the Pacific Railroad. Price made a feint toward St. Louis but turned west along the Missouri River.

Among the Union soldiers captured by Price at Pilot Knob were Major James Wilson and six men of the Third Cavalry MSM. Wilson and the Third Cavalry had a history, particularly with one of Price's regiments, the Fifteenth (Confederate) Missouri Cavalry, commanded by Colonel Timothy Reeves. Reeves and his men were sometime guerrillas. By 1863, Reeves, Wilson and their regiments repeatedly clashed in military operations that degenerated into what historian Mark Lause described as "a bitter war of reprisals." Guerrillas took few prisoners, and Federal commanders were chided if their captives were not "shot trying to escape."

The most spectacular—and controversial—action came in December 1863. On the twenty-third, Company C was building stables at Centreville when it was surprised by Reeves's cavalry. They gave up without a fight, and

Reeves started south with 102 prisoners. The mortified Federal commanders directed Major Wilson to take 200 men of the Third Cavalry from Pilot Knob and "to follow him to hell, and get the prisoners back." Wilson trailed them for two days, until he came upon Reeves's pickets about seventeen miles southwest of Doniphan.

Here the stories diverge. According to local Southern lore, Reeves, his men and a number of civilians were enjoying Christmas dinner at Pulliam's Farm when Wilson's cavalry burst in on them with guns blazing. Reeves's men returned fire, and then many fled. About thirty of his men were killed and more than one hundred captured. Southern writers say that Wilson proceeded to execute sixty-two women and children in what became known among them as the Pulliam Farm Massacre.

Union sources say that the Confederates were about to execute an officer and six men from Company C in retaliation for a similar execution of their men by William Leeper earlier that year. Just before the firing squad raised its guns, Wilson attacked. Union records and correspondence mention nothing about the presence of civilians or any civilian deaths.

Regardless of whether there was a civilian massacre at Pulliam's Farm, the action was a stinging defeat and, combined with retaliatory executions by both sides, created a greater than usual animosity between Reeves's men and the Third Cavalry. Thus, when Major Wilson, wounded, coatless and barefoot, fell into Confederate hands at Pilot Knob, he was rightly worried. He became more anxious a few days later when he and five others were singled out as members of the Third Cavalry and turned over to Colonel Reeves. Reeves took them to a nearby field and informed Wilson that they would be shot. "You do not mean to say that you are going to shoot us without a trial?" Wilson asked. "You have been tried," Reeves replied, "and such are my orders." Two volleys finished them off. There is no record of such a trial, but Reeves's apologists say there was one where Wilson was found guilty of killing civilians at the Pulliam Farm Massacre. Perhaps it was a drumhead court-martial, or perhaps it never happened.

The execution of Major Wilson became a cause célèbre for Missouri Unionists. Outraged Federal authorities selected six Confederate prisoners at random from the Gratiot Street Prison in St. Louis and executed them in retaliation. Lincoln intervened to prevent the execution of a Confederate major as part of the reprisal.

SAVED BY SHINPLASTERS

When Price made his left turn to go up the Missouri River, General Egbert Brown called in all the troops he could gather, much as he did at Springfield in January 1863. Among the 7,200 men summoned to Jefferson City were Company L and the Seventh Cavalry MSM.

While the bulk of Brown's force started digging entrenchments and building forts, the cavalry was ordered to guard the fords over the Osage River east of town as long as possible and then to fall back on the Moreau River—the last natural barrier before the Jefferson City fortifications—"contesting every inch of ground."

On October 6, Major Alexander Mullins patrolled the Osage with a battalion of the First Cavalry MSM. Mullins heard firing upstream and rode forward to engage the enemy on the Osage. Joining Mullins was a detachment of twelve men from the Seventh Cavalry led by Lieutenant George Houts, who had been on picket duty. The Federals drove Shelby's men out of a deep ravine and took cover there themselves. They called for reinforcements from the Seventh Cavalry, which had been held back as a reaction force. The fight became desperate as more and more Confederates crossed the river. After about twenty-five minutes, Mullins fell back. In the course of the firefight, Houts took a round to the face but lived. Mullins, joined by the rest of the Seventh Cavalry, stubbornly retreated to the Moreau. Somewhere in this fight, George Wolz's horse was wounded and died the next day.

October 7 opened with the Eighth Cavalry MSM fighting a series of rear-guard actions as it withdrew from the Moreau River to the defenses of Jefferson City. Price made a demonstration against the Union lines accompanied by artillery but no serious attack. With more vigor, and certainly had his army moved with more speed from Pilot Knob, he might have captured the state capital. That night, he decided to bypass the political plum of Jefferson City and move on to Boonville.

When the Seventh Cavalry, along with the other regiments at Jefferson City, were sent in pursuit of Price, Wolz was left behind without a horse. He gained another mount and, on October 20, rejoined his regiment near Lexington. A Federal army under Generals Samuel Curtis and James Blunt retreated before Price to the west, while Federal cavalry under General Alfred Pleasonton, a cavalry general sent from the Army of the Potomac, pressed Price from the east. The cavalry engaged Price's rear guard on the Little Blue River and in Independence on October 21. During this fight, guerrilla chieftain George Todd was mortally wounded.

On October 22, Blunt's men took up a position on the west bank of the Big Blue River. They resisted the Confederates' assault until their left flank was turned. Curtis and Blunt withdrew to Westport, and their fortified position on the Big Blue was occupied by Marmaduke's men. That evening, one of Pleasonton's brigades, led by Colonel Edward Winslow, exchanged gunfire with the Rebels across the Big Blue.

In the early morning of October 23, Pleasonton ordered Brown to move his three regiments—the First, Fourth and Seventh Cavalry MSM—to the fore, relieving Winslow. Dawn arrived, and Pleasonton found that Brown had not yet advanced. Pleasonton was furious. Shaking a cowhide whip in Brown's face, he cursed him for disobeying express orders. Pleasonton was known to have a low opinion of the Missouri militia, having fought against such shining lights as J.E.B. Stuart. Perhaps he was unaware, or did not care, that the Missouri State Militia was by then a collection of hardened veterans. For two and a half years, they fought small, but desperate, engagements against guerrillas who were every bit the match for Stuart's famed cavalry. Moreover, the loser of these engagements, more often than not, could expect no quarter. They certainly received little glory if they won.

Much to Lieutenant Colonel Lazear's delight, Pleasonton relieved both Brown and Colonel James McFerran on the spot. Colonel John Philips of the Seventh, who witnessed the scene while changing from his heavy cavalry boots to shoes more suitable for dismounted action, was appointed brigade commander in lieu of Brown. Lazear was ordered to take over the First Cavalry.

Philips's brigade moved to the east bank of the Big Blue River, where it took heavy fire from Marmaduke. He sent a party from the Fourth Cavalry to find a suitable crossing. A bit farther to the south, they found Byram's Ford, where the river was wide but fairly shallow. Wolz and his fellow soldiers dismounted and waded across the waist-deep river, holding their rifles and revolvers above their heads, to the woods on the other side. Marmaduke fell back to a long sloping hill. Two log cabins provided forts, and rail fences provided log breastworks, on the east side of which was an open field with stumps and rock outcroppings everywhere.

Philips's men rushed the hill but were driven to ground by devastating rifle and artillery fire. Wolz had faced small arms fire before, but this was the first serious artillery barrage the Seventh had seen in the war. Winslow's brigade followed Philips across the Big Blue and took up its position to his right. Winslow rode his horse up the slope, leading a charge by the Fourth Missouri, the Fourth Iowa Cavalry and the Tenth Missouri Volunteer

John Philips. Colonel Philips was the commander of the Seventh Cavalry MSM. He led the regiment and later a brigade at the Big Blue and Mine Creek. In 1883, Philips was Frank James's defense lawyer and obtained an acquittal for his client. Philips served as a congressman and was appointed a United States district judge for the Western District of Missouri in 1888. *Wilson's Creek National Battlefield.*

Cavalry. Sharpshooters in the trees at the top of the slope took aim and shot Winslow down, severely wounded in the leg. Lieutenant Colonel Frederick Benteen of the Tenth Missouri took over his brigade.

Lieutenant Colonel Crittenden, commanding the Seventh Cavalry after Philips's elevation, saw a Rebel sharpshooter in a tree level his rifle at him and fire. The ball struck Crittenden in the chest and knocked him to the ground. He felt for a wound but did not find one. It was deflected by a wad of Gamble shinplasters in his waistcoat.

The Federals once again swarmed up the hill, and this time they overpowered Marmaduke's men. Wolz wrote to his family that he got out his handgun to finish the fight. Some men in Winslow's regiments pumped round after round into the Rebel position with their sixteen-shot Henry repeating rifles, a weapon the Rebels described as that "Yankee rifle they load on Sunday and shoot all week."

Marmaduke fell back onto the prairie. A roar went up from Pleasonton's cavalry. The cheers were heard at Westport, where Curtis and Blunt were fighting Shelby. The contest was essentially over. The Confederates scrambled to get away and escaped with their wagon trains. But their escape was only temporary. Smelling blood, the Union troops hounded Price from Kansas City to the Arkansas line. At Mine Creek, on October 25, the Seventh Cavalry along with other regiments from Pleasonton's force conducted a classic cavalry charge—with sabers and revolvers—across the prairie and smashed the Rebel resistance. General Marmaduke, General John Cabell and several other high-ranking officers, as well as one thousand of their men, were captured. Most of their wagons were burned. Shelby fought two skillful rear-guard actions in the next few days, but Price's invasion had been decisively defeated.

With the defeat of Price and the killing of Bill Anderson and George Todd, the guerrilla war in Missouri limped to a conclusion. By November, Wolz was back in Warrensburg, where he had begun the campaign. The Seventh continued its patrolling but was mainly occupied in building huts and stables for the coming winter. The worst of the war was over.

Chapter 10

Mustering Out

In the first burst of patriotic enthusiasm, Federal ranks were quickly filled. But the setbacks and heavy casualties of 1862 slowed enlistments. The Federal government was desperate for men to replenish the armies in Virginia and Tennessee. In March 1863, it instituted the first national draft of the war, seeking 500,000 men to serve for three years or the duration. That was followed by draft calls in March, July and December 1864. The army's provost marshal, General James Fry, was in charge of recruitment. The local provost marshals sought out all male citizens aged twenty to forty-five to enroll them. Quotas were issued to the states, which in turn established quotas for each congressional district, as well as within the districts for towns. In the first two drafts, a person could avoid service by paying a $300 commutation fee. If actually drafted, one could pay a substitute to take one's place.

The process was convoluted. Potential draftees were "called" by a lottery. About 80 percent of those called reported, and about one-third were "held for service" (i.e., subject to being drafted). Of the remainder, 40 percent paid a commutation fee, and 35 percent obtained substitutes. During the war, the government announced that it was seeking 1.5 million men in the four draft calls. In the end, only 46,347 men were actually drafted.

The underlying purpose of the draft was not to conscript men into the army but rather to "encourage" them to volunteer. Volunteers and draftees were offered a $402 bounty that was often sweetened by their home state or home town to as much as $750—a huge sum at a time when privates

James Fry. General Fry was the provost marshal of the army. His duties included supervision of recruitment and the draft. Missouri officials frequently feuded with Fry over draft quotas, credits and recruitment policies. *Library of Congress*.

made $13 a month. But the desire to avoid service and the prospect of a fat payday encouraged abuses. Substitutes would join, take the money and disappear, only to pop up as a substitute for another man held to service. Brokers charged sometimes exorbitant fees to find substitutes. After the first draft, the government sought to crack down on fraud by paying only $100 when a man enlisted. He had to serve the full term to get the balance.

Even though the draft resulted in only a tiny number of men actually drafted—as opposed to volunteering, paying a commutation fee or obtaining a substitute—it was a political hot potato. There were draft riots in New York and protests elsewhere.

Missouri was not subject to the first two drafts. But when its turn came in July 1864, its politicians were among the loudest in their complaints. Although ultimately only 1,031 Missourians were actually drafted into service (it also supplied 1,638 substitutes), the protests were not unjustified. Unlike any other loyal state, Missouri had been and was still subject to a brutal guerrilla war. It had raised the Missouri State Militia specifically to deal with the guerrillas so that volunteer troops from Missouri and its neighboring states could be sent to fight the regular Confederate armies. Missouri had already subjected every loyal male to military service by requiring him to join the Enrolled Missouri Militia. Although conceived as a force that would only be called out in an emergency, many of these men served long periods on active duty with little or no pay. And the pay they did receive was not real money but "Gamble shinplasters," paper money in small denominations of little value, except to pay state taxes. July 1864 saw a resurgence of guerrilla violence, and the state was invaded by Price two months later. It is little wonder that Missouri politicians, Radical and Conservative, complained and that military commanders in the state recommended that the draft be suspended, at least until Price was dealt with.

A final draft call was issued in December 1864 requiring Missouri to supply 13,984 men, but circumstances in the state and the nation were changing. The Confederacy's collapse was clearly just a matter of time. Because of a sharp decline in guerrilla violence, the president quietly approved the lifting of martial law in Missouri in March 1865.

The Radical Republicans, led by Charles Drake, finally completed their rise to power in Missouri by a sweeping triumph in the 1864 elections. Drake had undergone a remarkable political transformation. He studied law with Hamilton Gamble before the war. He had been a Whig and an anti-foreigner Know-Nothing in the 1850s. He supported Claiborne Jackson in the 1860 election and spoke out against antislavery legislation into 1861.

Charles Drake. Drake was a St. Louis lawyer and former navy midshipman whose political ideas gravitated from the Know-Nothings in 1852 to Democratic supporter of secessionist Claiborne Jackson in 1860 to Radical Republicanism in 1863. He was the primary force behind the state constitution that abolished slavery in Missouri in January 1865; the document's punitive provisions earned it the name the "Drake Constitution." *Wilson's Creek National Battlefield.*

Thomas Fletcher. Fletcher was colonel of the Thirty-first Missouri Infantry. He was captured in December 1862 and spent five months in Libby Prison in Richmond, Virginia. Exchanged, he rejoined the regiment at the Siege of Vicksburg. He returned to Missouri in 1864. He raised and commanded the Forty-seventh Missouri Infantry at the Battle of Pilot Knob. He was elected governor in 1864 on the Radical Republican ticket. *Wilson's Creek National Battlefield.*

By 1863, though, Drake was a Radical, calling for immediate, uncompensated emancipation of slaves. He was now a foe of his former mentor, Governor Gamble. In October 1863, he led a delegation of seventy Missourians to a meeting with President Lincoln, whom he harangued for an hour with complaints about the president's policies and military commanders in the state. The Radicals initially opposed Lincoln's reelection but later united behind him when their favorite, John C. Frémont, withdrew from the race.

Drake's first major move was to spearhead a convention to write a new constitution. The president of the convention was Arnold Krekel, a Prussian-born lawyer and newspaperman from St. Charles (and, curiously for the times, an avowed agnostic). Krekel raised Home Guards early in the war and later commanded an independent battalion of the MSM. Both units were made up almost entirely of German Americans who considered almost any civilian in outstate Missouri a Secessionist sympathizer to be subjected to the roughest treatment. Typical of complaints against Krekel's men was a letter from a Callaway County man to Governor Gamble pointing out that while Krekel was eating dinner in the front yard, his soldiers were breaking in the house's back door and ransacking it. Krekel had no sympathy for his plight.

There were two major provisions Drake sought to have in the new state constitution: emancipation of the slaves and loyalty oaths to prevent former Confederates from having any power in the new government. On January 11, 1865, the constitutional convention adopted a provision that abolished slavery in the state effective July 4, 1865. The new constitution also contained a provision for an "iron-clad oath." No man could vote or serve as a public official, juror, lawyer, corporate officer, trustee, teacher or minister unless he signed an oath attesting that he had not committed any of eighty-six actions in support of the rebellion.

Shortly after taking office, new Governor Thomas Fletcher (a former brigade commander in Sherman's army) turned to military affairs. States could reduce the number of men subject to being drafted by being credited with those who were already in the service. The state's adjutant general had carried on an extensive correspondence with General Fry, quarreling about who could and could not be counted.

When the latest draft call came, Governor Fletcher proposed that the quotas be filled by raising six regiments of cavalry from veterans of the MSM for service within the state. Fry accepted the offer of six regiments but stipulated that they would be infantry regiments and available for service wherever the government needed them. Fletcher's appeal to Secretary

Stanton was rejected. Frustrated and afraid that the state would be stripped of an effective military presence, Fletcher acquiesced in the plan to raise six infantry regiments. They were never filled. On April 14, 1865, the War Department directed that all recruiting, including the draft, be ceased. Those Missouri men who had signed up in 1865 were all transferred to the Fifty-first Missouri Infantry. It never saw combat, but sadly, it lost forty-seven men to disease before it was mustered out.

In the meantime, the War Department sought to relieve the government of the burden of paying for militia regiments that it believed had served their purpose. Men such as George Wolz enlisted "for the war in Missouri." The department decided to interpret that phrase to mean "three years." And so the MSM was mustered out.

The Radicals quickly passed legislation dissolving the EMM, effective in March 1865. There was still a need for an armed Missouri-controlled force, and the legislature created another militia known simply as the Missouri Militia. There were familiar names, however, among the officers. William Leeper, disgraced as an officer during the war, was appointed colonel of the Twenty-fourth Regiment Missouri Militia. Arrow Rock's George Bingham was commissioned as a captain. This last iteration of Missouri militia served only a few months. Only fifty-eight companies were raised; all were mustered out by July 7, 1865. George Wolz was mustered out at Warrensburg on April 11, 1865.

Epilogue

At the end of the war, the MSM had 7,747 men under arms. According to the adjutant general, 14,265 men served in the MSM during the war, and 425 were killed in action or mortally wounded. Another 2,259 were discharged for disabilities, probably most for wounds received in battle, and 839 died of disease. This count does not include the men in the EMM, totaling at its height more than 52,000 men. How many of these men died or were wounded is not known; they served for short periods in units that kept few records (and those indifferently). There is no firm estimate of the number of soldiers, civilians and guerrillas who were casualties in the guerrilla war waged in the state. Even the records for soldiers are notoriously imprecise. Suffice it to say, it must have run into the thousands.

Most of the guerrillas took advantage of the amnesty offered to them. Dave Poole (after one last round of murders), accompanied by Henry Taylor, surrendered on May 20, 1865. He proceed to cooperate with Federal troops by going into the brush to convince his fellow guerrillas to come in and sign a loyalty oath. Most did so and tried to resume a normal life in postwar Missouri.

By 1870, the Radicals were out of office, the "iron-clad oath" had been declared unconstitutional and former Confederates were able to vote and hold office again. John Marmaduke was elected governor of Missouri in 1884. His immediate predecessor was Thomas Crittenden, one of his opponents on the Big Blue battlefield. Frank James, the former guerrilla and postwar train and bank robber, surrendered to Crittenden in the governor's office in Jefferson City in 1882. He was tried and acquitted of murder by a jury in Gallatin, Missouri. His defense counsel was John Philips, the former colonel of the Seventh Cavalry MSM.

Bazel Lazear moved to Auxvasse, Missouri, after the war. He was appointed postmaster and carried on a lengthy but unsuccessful fight to get a pension for his wartime injuries, probably a double inguinal hernia he suffered during the campaign against Price.

Bugler William Caton married Julia Blankemeister, a student at the Boonville Female Academy. They moved to Winfield, Kansas, where William owned a successful marble works. Julia was an accomplished musician and a leader in the Woman's Christian Temperance Union. William died in 1943 at the age of ninety-four.

Ludwick St. John also survived the war. He was so enamored of the military life (and perhaps the reenlistment bounty) that he joined the Thirty-ninth Missouri Volunteer Infantry just a few days after being mustered out of the Ninth Cavalry in 1865. Upon his discharge from the infantry later that year, St. John may have returned to his Boone County home, but his military career was not over. St. John enlisted in the Seventh United States Cavalry in 1869. He was killed with Custer in the Battle of the Little Bighorn on June 25, 1876.

George Wolz returned to Grundy County. He and his brother, John, married sisters. George became a prosperous farmer, owner of a Texas cattle ranch and part owner of a bank. George built a beautiful home in Trenton, Missouri. Wolz died on June 18, 1924, at the age of eighty-two. In the obituary, he was remembered simply as "A Union Veteran."

Bibliography

Adams, George Worthington. *Doctors in Blue: The Medical History of the Union Army in the Civil War*. Baton Rouge: Louisiana University Press, 1952.

Annual Report of the Adjutant General of Missouri, 1865. Jefferson City, MO: Emory S. Foster, Public Printer, 1866.

Baird, Samuel. *With Merrill's Cavalry: The Civil War Experience of Samuel Baird, 2ⁿᵈ Missouri Cavalry, U.S.A.* San Marcos, CA: Book Habit, 1981.

Banasik, Michael E. *Cavaliers of the Brush: Quantrill and His Men*. Iowa City, IA: Camp Pope Bookshop, 2003.

Bartlett, Dr. Aurelius T. *Order Book and Letter Book*. Aurelius T. Bartlett Collection. St. Louis: Missouri History Museum, 1862–96.

Beilein, Joseph M., Jr. "'The Presence of These Families Is the Cause of the Presence There of the Guerrillas': The Influence of Little Dixie Households on the Civil War in Missouri." Master's thesis, University of Missouri, 2006.

Benecke, Louis. *Historical Sketch of the "Sixties."* Brunswick, MO, 1909.

Bilby, Joseph G. *Civil War Firearms: Their Historical Background and Tactical Use and Modern Collecting and Shooting.* Conshohocken, PA: Combined Books, 1996.

Boman, Dennis K. *Lincoln and Citizens' Rights in Civil War Missouri: Balancing Freedom and Security.* Baton Rouge: Louisiana State University Press, 2011.

Bordewich, Fergus M. *America's Great Debate: Henry Clay, Stephen A. Douglas, and the Compromise that Preserved the Union.* New York: Simon and Schuster, 2012.

Britton, Wiley. *The Civil War on the Border.* 2 vols. New York: G.P. Putnam's Sons, 1899.

Brownlee, Richard S. *Gray Ghosts of the Confederacy: Guerrilla War in the West 1861–1865.* Baton Rouge: Louisiana University Press, 1986.

Buffon, Dianne, and Linda Brown-Kubisch, eds. *Report of the Committee of the House of Representatives of the General Assembly of the State of Missouri Appointed to Investigate the Conduct and Management of the Militia, Including an Index.* Columbia: State Historical Society of Missouri, 1998.

Canan, Howard V. "Milton Burch, Anti-Guerrilla Fighter." *Missouri Historical Review* 59 (January 1965): 223.

———. "The Missouri Paw Paw Militia of 1863–1864." *Missouri Historical Review* 62 (July 1968): 431.

Castel, Albert. *General Sterling Price and the Civil War in the West.* Baton Rouge: Louisiana State University Press, 1968.

———. "Order No. 11 and the Civil War on the Border." *Missouri Historical Review* 57 (1963): 357.

Castel, Albert, and Tom Goodrich. *Bloody Bill Anderson: The Short, Savage Life of a Civil War Guerrilla.* Lawrence: University Press of Kansas, 1998.

Cozzens, Peter, and Robert I. Girardi, eds. *The Military Memoirs of General John Pope.* Chapel Hill: University of North Carolina Press, 1998.

Donald, David Herbert. *Charles Sumner and the Coming of the Civil War*. New York: Alfred A. Knopf, 1967.

———. *Lincoln*. New York: Simon and Schuster, 1996.

Ehlmann, Steve. *Crossroads: A History of St. Charles County, Missouri*. St. Charles, MO: Lindenwood University Press, 2011.

Fehrenbacher, Don E. *The Dred Scott Case: Its Significance in American Law and Politics*. New York: Oxford University Press, 1978.

Fellman, Michael. *Inside War: The Guerrilla Conflict in Missouri During the American Civil War*. New York: Oxford University Press, 1989.

Filbert, Preston. *The Half Not Told: The Civil War in a Frontier Town*. Mechanicsburg, PA: Stackpole Books, 2001.

Ford, James Everitt. *History of Grundy County*. Trenton, MO: News Publishing Company, 1908.

Frizzell, Robert W. "'Killed By Rebels': A Civil War Massacre And Its Aftermath." *A Rough Business: Fighting the Civil War in Missouri*. Edited by William Garrett Piston. Columbia: State Historical Society of Missouri, 2012.

Fyfer, J. Thomas. *History of Boone County*. St. Louis: Western Historical Company, 1882.

Geary, James W. *We Need Men: The Union Draft in the Civil War*. DeKalb: Northern Illinois University Press, 1991.

Gerteis, Louis S. *The Civil War in Missouri: A Military History*. Columbia: University of Missouri Press, 2012.

Gilmore, Donald L. *Civil War on the Missouri-Kansas Border*. New York: Pelican Publishing Company, 2008.

Goodrich, Thomas. *Black Flag: Guerrilla Warfare on the Western Border, 1861–1865*. Bloomington: Indiana University Press, 1999.

Hamilton, James A. "The Enrolled Missouri Militia: Its Creation and Controversial History." *Missouri Historical Review* 69 (July 1975): 422.

Harris, Charles F. "Catalyst for Terror: The Collapse of the Women's Prison in Kansas City." *Missouri Historical Review* 89 (1995): 290.

Harris, William C. *Lincoln and the Border States*. Lawrence: University Press of Kansas, 2011.

History of Lafayette County, Missouri. St. Louis: Missouri Historical Company, 1881.

Holcombe, Return I. *History of Greene County*. St. Louis, MO: Western Historical Company, 1883.

Horwitz, Tony. *Midnight Rising: John Brown and the Raid that Sparked the Civil War*. New York: Henry Holt and Company, 2011.

Houts, Joseph K., Jr. *Quantrill's Thieves*. Kansas City, MO: Truman Publishing Company, 2002.

Inspector General's Report, December 31, 1863. Reprinted in *Journal of the Senate of Missouri, Twenty-Second General Assembly* (1863).

Jenkins, Paul B. *The Battle of Westport*. Kansas City, MO: Franklin Hudson Publishing Company, 1906.

Launer, Louis J. "Arnold Krekel." *St. Charles Heritage* 16 (April 1998): 38.

Lause, Mark A. *Price's Lost Campaign: The 1864 Invasion of Missouri*. Columbia: University of Missouri Press, 2011.

Leopard, Burl, and Floyd Shoemaker, eds. *The Messages and Proclamations of the Governors of the State of Missouri*. Vol. 3. Columbia: State Historical Society of Missouri, 1922.

Leslie, Edward E. *The Devil Knows How to Ride: The True Story of William Clarke Quantrill and His Confederate Raiders*. New York: Random House, 1996.

Lothrop, Charles A. *A History of the First Regiment Iowa Cavalry, Veteran Volunteers.* Lyons, IA: Beers & Eaton, Printers, 1890.

Lundstrom, John B. *One Drop in a Sea of Blue.* St. Paul: Minnesota Historical Society Press, 2012.

Malone, Dumas. *Jefferson and His Time.* Vol. 6. *The Sage of Monticello.* Boston: Little, Brown and Company, 1981.

McAuley, John D. *Carbines of the Civil War, 1861–1865.* Union City, TN: Pioneer Press, 1981.

McLarty, Vivian Kirkpatrick. "The Civil War Letters of Colonel Bazel F. Lazear." Part I. *Missouri Historical Review* 44 (April 1950): 254.

———. "The Civil War Letters of Colonel Bazel F. Lazear." Part II. *Missouri Historical Review* 44 (July 1950): 387.

———. "The Civil War Letters of Colonel Bazel F. Lazear." Part III. *Missouri Historical Review* 45 (October 1950): 47.

Million, John W. *State Aid to Railways in Missouri.* Chicago, IL: University of Chicago Press, 1896.

Mountbank, Clay. *Punitive War: Confederate Guerrillas and Union Reprisals.* Lawrence: University Press of Kansas, 2009.

Mudd, Joseph A. *With Porter in North Missouri: A Chapter in the History of the War Between the States.* Washington, D.C.: National Publishing Company, 1909.

Murdock, Eugene C. *One Million Men: The Civil War Draft in the North.* Madison: State Historical Society of Wisconsin, 1971.

Nagel, Paul C. *George Caleb Bingham: Missouri's Famed Painter and Forgotten Politician.* Columbia: University of Missouri Press, 2005.

National Archives and Records Administration. *Compiled Service Records of Volunteer Union Soldiers Who Served in Organizations from the State of Missouri.* Record Group 94. Microfilm, M405, various reels. Washington, D.C.

Neely, Jeremy. *The Border Between Them: Violence and Reconciliation on the Kansas-Missouri Line*. Columbia: University of Missouri Press, 2007.

Nichols, Bruce. *Guerrilla Warfare in Civil War Missouri, 1862*. Jefferson, NC: McFarland & Company Inc., 2004.

———. *Guerrilla Warfare in Civil War Missouri*. Vol. 2. *1863*. Jefferson, NC: McFarland & Company Inc., 2007.

Nichols, Ronald, ed. *Men with Custer: Biographies of the 7th Cavalry*. Hardin, MT: Custer Battlefield & Historical Association Inc., 2010.

Parrish, William A. *Missouri Under Radical Rule, 1865–1870*. Columbia: University of Missouri Press, 1965.

———. *Turbulent Partnership: Missouri and the Union 1861–1865*. Columbia: University of Missouri Press, 1963.

Phillips, Christopher. *Damned Yankee: The Life of General Nathaniel Lyon*. Columbia: University of Missouri Press, 1990.

———. *Missouri's Confederate: Claiborne Fox Jackson and the Creation of Southern Identity in the Border West*. Columbia: University of Missouri Press, 2000.

Piston, William Garrett, and Thomas P. Sweeney. *Portraits of Conflict: A Photographic History of Missouri in the Civil War*. Fayetteville: University of Arkansas Press, 2009.

Report of the North Missouri Railroad Company. Appendix. "Exhibit B." Reprinted in *Journal of the Senate of Missouri, Twenty-Second General Assembly* (1863).

Ross, Kirby, ed. *Autobiography of Samuel S. Hildebrand: The Renowned Missouri Bushwhacker*. Fayetteville: University of Arkansas reprint, 2005. Originally published in 1871.

Sawyer v. Hannibal & St. Joseph R. Co. 37 Mo. 240 (1866).

Schrantz, Ward L. *Jasper County, Missouri, in the Civil War*. Reprint. Carthage: Carthage, Missouri Kiwanis Club, 1988.

Sellmeyer, Deryl P. *Jo Shelby's Iron Brigade.* Gretna, LA: Pelican Publishing Company, 2007.

Sheridan, Richard B. "From Slavery in Missouri to Freedom in Kansas: The Influx of Black Fugitives and Contrabands into Kansas, 1854–1865." *Kansas History* 12 (1989): 28.

Sigmund, Judy. *Dog Prairie Tales.* 2nd ed. St. Charles, MO: Goellner Printing Company, 2005.

Starr, Stephen Z. "Cavalry Tactics in the Civil War." Cincinnati Civil War Round Table, April 26, 1959. Available at www.cincinnaticwrt.org/data/ccwrt_history/talks_text/starr_cavalry_tactics.html.

———. *The Union Cavalry in the Civil War.* Vol. 1. *From Fort Sumter to Gettysburg.* Baton Rouge: Louisiana State University Press, 1979.

———. *The Union Cavalry in the Civil War.* Vol. 3. *The War in the West, 1861–1865.* Baton Rouge: Louisiana State University Press, 2007.

Stiles, T.J. *Jesse James: Last Rebel of the Civil War.* New York: Vintage, 2003.

Sturgeon, Isaac N. *"Reminiscences," in Isaac H. Sturgeon Papers.* St. Louis: Missouri History Museum, 1861–1902.

Tucker, Philip Thomas. *The Forgotten "Stonewall of the West": Major General John Stevens Bowen.* Macon, GA: Mercer University Press, 1997.

The War of the Rebellion: A Compilation of the Official Records of the Union and Confederate Armies. Washington, D.C.: United States Government Printing Office, 1880–1901.

Whites, Leeann. "Forty Shirts and a Wagonload of Wheat: Women, the Domestic Supply Line, and the Civil War on the Western Border." *Journal of the Civil War Era* 1 (2011): 56.

Whittaker, Frederick. *Volunteer Cavalry: The Lessons of the Decade.* New York, 1871.

Winter, William C. *The Civil War in St. Louis: A Guided Tour*. St. Louis: Missouri Historical Society Press, 1994.

Wolz, George. *George Wolz Letters*. St. Louis: Missouri History Museum, 1862–64.

Woodhead, Henry, ed. *Echoes of Glory: Arms and Equipment of the Union*. Alexandria, VA: Time-Life Books, 1991.

Index

About the Author

James W. Erwin is a Missouri native. He graduated from Missouri State University with a BA in mathematics. After service in the United States Army, he obtained an MA in history from the University of Missouri and a JD from the University of Missouri Law School. He has practiced law in St. Louis for more than thirty-six years. Mr. Erwin is married to Vicki Berger Erwin. They live in Kirkwood, Missouri.